Ultimate
Grilling Cookbook

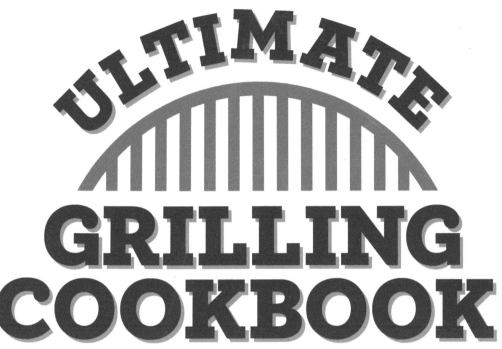

ULTIMATE GRILLING COOKBOOK

Everything You Need to Know to Master Your Gas or Charcoal Grill

Derrick Riches and Sabrina Baksh

ROCKRIDGE
PRESS

For Zoë

First Rockridge Press trade paperback edition 2022

Rockridge Press and the Rockridge Press logo are trademarks or registered trademarks of Callisto Media Inc. and/or its affiliates in the United States and other countries and may not be used without written permission.

For general information on our other products and services, please contact our Customer Care Department within the United States at (866) 744-2665, or outside the United States at (510) 253-0500.

Paperback ISBN: 978-1-68539-139-3 | ebook ISBN: 978-1-68539-392-2

Manufactured in the United States of America

Interior and Cover Designer: Mando Daniel
Art Producer: Maya Melenchuk
Editor: Georgia Freedman
Production Editor: Matthew Burnett
Production Manager: Martin Worthington

Photography © Ian Bagwell, pp. ii, viii, 82, 120, 158; © Marija Vidal pp. 16, 58; © Andrew Purcell, p. 86; © Thomas J. Story, pp. 104, 128, 144; © Monica Buck, p. 112; © Darren Muir, pp. vii, 134, 154. Food styling by Karen Shinto, p. 144. All other images used under license from Shutterstock and iStock. Author photograph of Derrick Riches courtesy of Newton Photography (Utah); author photograph of Sabrina Baksh courtesy of Derrick Riches.

10 9 8 7 6 5 4 3 2 1 0

Contents

Introduction

The very foundation of human civilization began with a simple spark. Since its discovery, the element of fire has provided warmth, safety, and a pathway to nourishment for humanity. In the modern world, we've created a convenient, contained structure to harness this pure, ancient form of cooking. The backyard grill, whether charcoal or gas, offers both incredible convenience and endless culinary possibilities. We have written this book to explore those possibilities, and we hope you are ready to join us on that incredible journey.

For nearly two decades, we (Derrick and Sabrina) have worked together to develop tasty, easy-to-follow recipes for the outdoor cooking enthusiast. Derrick has written about barbecue and grilling since 1997, and he has cooked on every conceivable type of cooking equipment, from the most expensive grills and smokers to a pile of coals in the ground. Sabrina has explored the world of live-fire cooking using a global culinary perspective. Together, we bring our experience and know-how to help you get the most out of your grill. We have co-authored multiple smoking and grilling cookbooks and work closely on developing enjoyable and informative barbecue content for DerrickRiches.com.

Although this book contains 101 delicious recipes, its true purpose is to offer you a lesson in grilling basics. We start with an in-depth course in grills and grilling, guiding you through everything from two-zone fires to smoke production, searing, and low-and-slow roasting. We also discuss grill specifications and accessories, so your next purchase will be informed—and fulfilling. Once you have a handle on your tool kit, we turn to the recipes. Want to make spareribs on your grill? We show you how to do it without a smoker and still infuse them with smoky flavor. Want a filet mignon that rivals the best steak houses or perfectly flaky fish? We've got you covered.

We hit the four major protein categories—beef, fish, pork, and poultry—detailing how to cook all the major cuts. We also explore global and fusion cuisine, including dishes such as Gochujang Chicken (page 48) and Tandoori Rack of Lamb (page 110). And don't worry, there are plenty of side dishes and vegetables to complete your menu.

We firmly believe that grilling can be easy and rewarding. Armed with the right tips, tricks, and recipes, you'll be inspired to grill year-round and cook for weeknight dinners, weekend get-togethers, and special occasions.

Contents

Introduction

The very foundation of human civilization began with a simple spark. Since its discovery, the element of fire has provided warmth, safety, and a pathway to nourishment for humanity. In the modern world, we've created a convenient, contained structure to harness this pure, ancient form of cooking. The backyard grill, whether charcoal or gas, offers both incredible convenience and endless culinary possibilities. We have written this book to explore those possibilities, and we hope you are ready to join us on that incredible journey.

For nearly two decades, we (Derrick and Sabrina) have worked together to develop tasty, easy-to-follow recipes for the outdoor cooking enthusiast. Derrick has written about barbecue and grilling since 1997, and he has cooked on every conceivable type of cooking equipment, from the most expensive grills and smokers to a pile of coals in the ground. Sabrina has explored the world of live-fire cooking using a global culinary perspective. Together, we bring our experience and know-how to help you get the most out of your grill. We have co-authored multiple smoking and grilling cookbooks and work closely on developing enjoyable and informative barbecue content for DerrickRiches.com.

Although this book contains 101 delicious recipes, its true purpose is to offer you a lesson in grilling basics. We start with an in-depth course in grills and grilling, guiding you through everything from two-zone fires to smoke production, searing, and low-and-slow roasting. We also discuss grill specifications and accessories, so your next purchase will be informed—and fulfilling. Once you have a handle on your tool kit, we turn to the recipes. Want to make spareribs on your grill? We show you how to do it without a smoker and still infuse them with smoky flavor. Want a filet mignon that rivals the best steak houses or perfectly flaky fish? We've got you covered.

We hit the four major protein categories—beef, fish, pork, and poultry—detailing how to cook all the major cuts. We also explore global and fusion cuisine, including dishes such as Gochujang Chicken (page 48) and Tandoori Rack of Lamb (page 110). And don't worry, there are plenty of side dishes and vegetables to complete your menu.

We firmly believe that grilling can be easy and rewarding. Armed with the right tips, tricks, and recipes, you'll be inspired to grill year-round and cook for weeknight dinners, weekend get-togethers, and special occasions.

CHAPTER ONE

The Great Wide World of Grilling

Grills come in every shape and size, yet they all work pretty much the same way. Because of this, grilling is easy, and switching between different styles of grills doesn't mean relearning everything. And, yes, there are many grill styles beyond the simple choice of gas or charcoal (more on that later).

In this chapter, you'll get the lowdown on the major types of grills, then learn about the accessories you need and the ones to avoid—because having the right tools can make a world of difference to your process and results. Finally, you'll learn about our favorite must-have pantry items— the ones that will become your staples for successful grilling.

Get Fired Up for Grilled Flavor

Burgers, chicken, chops, and hot dogs have always been Americans' favorite items to cook on a grill. Although a grill's potential far exceeds these obvious choices, we want to help you take these popular grilled foods to a whole new level while opening you up to the diverse and wide world of live-fire cooking.

The often-overlooked vegetable is one of the easiest items to grill. In fact, we think that the grill is the perfect cooking equipment for vegetables. The flavors aren't boiled away, and the fire's smokiness enhances both fruits and vegetables in ways that a stovetop or oven simply can't match.

When most people approach the grill, they think of direct-flame quick cooking. But most grills can also perform indirect, low-and-slow cooking. This means that your holiday roast, Sunday chicken, or cheesecake dessert can be cooked on the grill safely and effectively. And when you add wood chips or chunks to your gas or charcoal grill, you can also give most foods a smoky flavor.

Grilling is also one of the most common cooking methods worldwide. Although grills in places like Japan, Laos, and Mexico might look different than the ones we have in our backyards in the United States, they work similarly. Along with classic Western recipes, we share our favorite global recipes and explain how to adapt them to your grill.

Firing up a grill is one of our favorite things to do, and we're excited to share our years of knowledge with you. Whether your grill is powered by charcoal or gas, this book will help you expand your outdoor cooking skills in every way. You'll see quickly that although upping your grilling game will give you the ability to cook for every occasion, it doesn't make the process more complicated.

5 Things to Know Before Grilling

There are a few rules for safe, successful grilling that we need to address. Outdoor cooking is not as predictable as turning on your oven. Weather, daylight, and the size of your gathering will have an impact on how you cook. You need to be prepared, particularly when you are grilling foods that cook fast. With these foods, a minute or two can make the difference between a medium-rare steak and a charred piece of beef.

1. **Have extra fuel on hand.** You have everything prepared. The food is on the grill, but suddenly your fire dies. It happens. And this problem isn't just limited to gas grills. Charcoal grills can also burn through your charcoal supply mid-cookout. Keep a spare propane tank on hand for your gas grill and a charcoal chimney and extra charcoal ready for your charcoal unit.

2. **Keep your grill away from flammable items.** Your grill manual has a section that shows how far your grill needs to be placed from structures and trees. Always follow these guidelines. It is also best to place your grill away from foot traffic. A knocked-over grill can be a huge disaster.

3. **Make sure everything you need is nearby.** When grilling, you should have everything you need close at hand. Running inside for an extra plate or a basting sauce can mean taking your eyes off the food long enough for it to burn. If possible, enlist a helper so you can stay focused on cooking.

4. **Be prepared.** Flare-ups and fires can happen. The best solution is to quickly move food out of the way, then let the fire die down. Spraying water on a grease fire is dangerous and doesn't solve the problem. The grease will remain in the grill. By moving the food, you eliminate the fuel for the flare-up so it will die away naturally.

5. **Keep an eye on the wind.** For most grills, cold weather, rain, or snow won't seriously affect outdoor cooking. On the other hand, wind can fan a fire to extreme temperatures or pull the heat right out of your grill. Wind can also blow out gas burners on a low setting. Being aware of the wind will help you minimize these problems. If possible, move your grill to a safe sheltered space to reduce these effects.

The Lowdown on Gas Grills

Gas grills have been around for decades. They first appeared in backyards in the 1950s, and by the late 1980s, they had become the most popular style of outdoor cooking equipment. The biggest reason they're so popular is that they are nearly as easy to use as an oven or stovetop. A modern gas grill is more akin to a kitchen appliance than to a charcoal grill.

Gas grills can burn either propane or natural gas and are available in a wide range of prices and with a variety of features. Some may come with side burners similar to a stovetop burner. Others have rotisserie burners or the option for adding a specialized tool for rotisserie cooking.

You can also use griddles inside your grill for cooking eggs and pancakes. And there are several grill toppers for cooking vegetables and other small items. In fact, there are too many accessories to count. Suffice it to say, if there's a food you want to cook, there is a tool out there to help you cook it on your gas grill.

What to Know

Gas grills come in a wide range of prices, styles, and configurations. When buying a gas grill, know that you can spend anywhere from a few hundred to several thousand dollars. And this doesn't include the added accessories (some gas grills are practically buried in these extras).

Start your gas grill shopping with a price range in mind, and then look for a standard grill that fits your needs in terms of size and capacity. Most people purchase large grills, but these burn through fuel faster and take longer to reach optimal temperature, and many home cooks don't need the extra space. We recommend a three-burner gas grill. They are much more versatile and allow you to cook indirectly. A unit with more than four burners is overkill for most people.

Next, add the extras you want, such as a side burner, rotisserie system, or sear burners. The gas grills worth buying have a basic version and a deluxe version. Most people won't use high-end model features, so consider them only if you're certain you will use them. We prefer to keep our accessories simple but durable.

One last piece of buying advice: Never buy a gas grill that is only available through one retailer. These are almost always inferior grills.

Pros

Convenience is the number one reason for buying a gas grill. They are easy to use and reliable. Most people love their gas grill because you can light it in seconds and be ready to cook in as little as 10 minutes. There are no vents to adjust; just set the dials to your desired temperature and you are ready to grill.

Gas grills are also considered self-cleaning. Although this isn't entirely true (it still takes some work), the process is relatively easy: Preheat the grill to its highest setting, use a grill cleaning tool to scrape off the grates, and your grill is food-safe for cooking (see Cleanup and Care, page 5). Because of this feature, you can come home from work and be ready to grill in less than 15 minutes, because you don't have to worry about cleaning out ash and leftover charcoal. Once you're done cooking, simply turn off the grill and the gas supply.

Cons

The biggest limitation of a gas grill is that it doesn't produce many of the kinds of flavors you typically associate with grilling. This is because burning propane or natural gas does not produce smoke, as burning charcoal or hardwood does. If you want to achieve a smoky flavor while using a gas grill, you will need to make the smoke in a different way (see Smoking, page 26). And even the best smoke-making methods won't give you the same flavor as a charcoal grill or smoker.

There is also a limitation regarding the versatility of most gas grills. The burners sit well below the cooking grates, and there are metal plates between the fire and the food. These protect the burners and even out the heat but they also limit the heat your grill can produce. A charcoal grill with the right setup can sear at higher temperatures than a gas grill.

Cleanup and Care

Although you may not need to clean ash from a gas grill, you do need to do some work—a clean gas grill is a happy gas grill. Dirty grills produce foul flavors and do not burn evenly. Worse, a dirty grill will cause more flare-ups that burn your food.

Your grill manual has information about cleaning your specific model, but here are some general rules for keeping your gas grill clean:

1. **Always preheat your gas grill to its highest temperature.** Doing this will help burn off any germs and grease inside your grill.

2. **Clean your cooking grates before and after you cook.** Clean cooking grates help prevent foods from sticking and give you better contact between your food and the metal of the grate for heat transfer. We recommend nonwire bristle grill cleaning tools (see Grill Cleaning Tool, page 12, for our favorite).

3. **Empty your grease tray frequently.** Most gas grills collect drippings and grease in a tray under the grill. We recommend disposable aluminum foil pans that fit into the grease tray for collecting grease and removing it every five cookouts. This makes cleanup a breeze and most grill makers either sell or have a recommended size of foil pan that fits the tray correctly.

4. **Do a deep clean of your grill after every three months of use.** A deep clean means removing the grill's cooking grates and flame tamers (those metal plates that sit above the burners), then getting inside the grill to clean off food debris and grease. There are several grill degreasers on the market; this is the time to use them. We like Goo Gone Grill & Grate Cleaner, which can be found with the grilling products in your grocery store.

PROPANE KNOW-HOW

You never want to run out of propane in the middle of a cookout. The solution is to keep an extra, full propane tank on hand. Swap it in when the tank you're using is empty, then have the empty one refilled. If you make this a habit, you will never be left searching for propane in the middle of a cookout.

When it comes time to refill the tank, we recommend a refilling station over propane tank exchange programs. It might not be as convenient, but it is considerably more economical. A quick internet search will help you find a refilling station in your area.

Propane tanks need to be stored in a well-ventilated location. They also need to be kept out of the sun and away from any area with an open flame. Do not store a new propane tank inside or near your gas grill.

How to Fire It Up

Before turning on the grill, turn on the gas supply. Ensure that all valves are in the off position. Now, lift the lid, turn on the main burners, and push the ignition button. Listen for the "whoosh" and look for the flames. Check to see that all the burners are lit. Now you can close the lid and let the grill preheat.

What do you do if your grill doesn't light? Dangling off the back of your grill is a piece of wire on a chain. This piece holds a match to light your grill if the igniter button doesn't work. That said, we're not fond of these, because they are awkward to use and the match always blows out before you can get it to the burner. It's better to use a fireplace match or a long-reach lighter; always use caution when lighting your grill.

Remember, if your grill does not light in the first 10 seconds, turn off the valves and the gas from the source. Leave the lid open and allow the gas inside the grill to dissipate for five minutes before attempting to light it again.

One last, important note: Most gas grills leak a tiny bit, and a tiny leak can drain a full propane tank in about a month. To conserve fuel—and for safety's sake—always turn off your gas grill's fuel supply at the source. This holds true for both propane and natural gas grills.

The Lowdown on Charcoal Grills

Charcoal grills emerged in the 1920s but exploded in popularity in the 1950s. Today, there are many charcoal grills on the market, ranging from simple hibachi-style grills to computer-controlled marvels. This book is designed to suit most of these different units, but to grill indirectly (something you'll need to do for a number of our recipes), you'll need a grill with a lid.

The most classic charcoal grill is a freestanding unit with a separate lid. There are vents in the lid and the bottom of the grill's body. The bottom vent allows air into the grill, whereas the top vent limits the amount of air escaping from the grill. By adjusting these vents, you control the heat inside the grill. A good charcoal grill can cook at temperatures that range from just under 200°F to more than 700°F.

The vents also control the amount of smoke held inside the grill. The smoke will remain in the grill longer when the top vent is partially closed and the bottom vent is opened fairly wide. Most charcoal grills can be good smokers; some, like larger kettle grills and kamado grills, make excellent smokers.

A charcoal grill seems simple, but it is much more versatile than a gas grill (see our Pros list, page 8). These units also last much longer if they are well maintained.

What to Know

There is more variety in charcoal grill styles than in gas grills. You can find simple metal grills for $100 that will do a great job, or you can spend well over $1,000 on a kamado unit that is both a good grill and a great smoker. Usually, cheaper charcoal grills don't come with a lot of extras, although the more popular models do offer a variety of accessories.

What we like about a good charcoal grill is its simplicity. These grills are not meant to replace your kitchen or perform like a modern appliance. Charcoal cooking harkens back to the past and is more about the artistry of cooking. Charcoal grilling is an experience.

When shopping for a charcoal grill, don't buy the first product you find at the hardware store. There are cheap and ineffective charcoal grills out there that will simply rust away in a few years. Look for name brands that have been in the business for a while. We like the Weber Kettle for its versatility and the Big Green Egg for its amazing cooking capabilities. There is a large price gap between the two, and lots of models within those two price points, so do your research before purchasing (see Resources, page 174).

Pros

The biggest advantage of a charcoal grill is the flavor it creates. Ask any charcoal griller why they prefer their grill, and they will say it's the smoky goodness imbued into the food. You can further enhance that smoke flavor by adding wood chunks to the fire. And with so many great hardwoods available, you can pick and choose the smoke profile to match your food.

Additionally, charcoal grills can be much more versatile once you master the art of fire building. You can bank coals to one side for indirect smoking, roasting, or intense searing. In a good-size charcoal grill, you can roast chicken and grill steaks simultaneously as long as you keep the lid on as much as possible.

Cons

The downside to charcoal grills is the work. They take longer to light (which we talk about in the next section) and require more skill to master than a gas grill. Also, you need to clean out the ash after every use. All of this means that a charcoal grill requires a greater investment in time and energy than a gas grill.

Charcoal can also be more temperamental than gas. Even the most experienced griller has had that fire that just won't light. Yes, there are accessories to make this easier, but you don't generally light a charcoal grill with the push of a button. Add a good dose of wind, and you might have some difficulty getting your charcoal grill burning. You'll need to be patient with this style of cooking.

How to Fire It Up

You might have heard that the first rule of lighting charcoal is to avoid lighter fluid. You will find this rule in every cookbook and website. But it isn't entirely true. Today, many all-natural lighter fluids burn clean and leave no residue on foods. However, petroleum-based lighter fluids and self-lighting charcoal are definite no-nos.

We light our charcoal in a chimney, a metal cylinder that lights charcoal cleanly and quickly. You can buy a good charcoal chimney for around $30. The best part of owning a chimney is that you can light charcoal outside the grill, then dump it onto the coal grate when it is ready. This makes the chimney indispensable if you need to replenish the charcoal in your grill during a long cookout.

We also use natural lighter cubes. These are small, wax-based blocks that light easily and burn hot. Simply place them in the grill, light them, and surround them with charcoal. They are quick, cheap, and very useful to get your fire started.

The important thing about lighting charcoal isn't the method—it's the timing. Light your charcoal grill early. You can add more charcoal or wood before your food goes on, but you won't be waiting for the fire. Let the fire wait for you. This also gives you time to adjust the vents to maintain your target temperature easily.

Cleanup and Care

Charcoal and ash are dirty, so many people assume that cleaning a charcoal grill is a dirty job. With most modern charcoal grills, this isn't the case as, generally, most have ash catchers, drawers, or access doors to the ashes. After every cook, it is important to remove the ash once the grill has completely cooled down.

One thing to know about charcoal grills is that you don't have to discard unused charcoal. At the end of each cookout, close all the vents. This will snuff the fire. The remaining charcoal can be reused unless it has been sitting for a month or exposed to moisture.

You should use a grill cleaning tool (see page 12) as opposed to a wire bristle brush to clean the cooking grates before and after each cookout. You should also bring the grill up to a high temperature (above 165°F) and leave it at that heat level for 10 minutes before cooking to ensure that the cooking surface is sterile.

Once you are done cooking, close the vents and let the grill cool for at least 12 hours before cleaning out ash and food debris. Every few months (or every 10 cookouts), remove everything inside the grill and give it a thorough cleaning. Remember, a clean grill is a happy grill. And a dirty grill will add unpleasant flavors to your food.

BRIQUETTES VERSUS LUMP CHARCOAL

Charcoal comes in two main varieties: briquette and lump.

Most people are familiar with the bags of charcoal briquettes found everywhere. This charcoal is made from sawdust. That sawdust is placed into a low-oxygen furnace and turned into char. It is then mixed with a binder (basically sugar) and formed into uniform pillow shapes.

Lump charcoal is made from wood scraps, from either cut wood lumber or pieces of tree branches. It is fired in a kiln without oxygen and turned into charcoal. Lump is not uniform, and each bag will have small and large pieces.

Barbecue purists tend to favor lump, but the choice is up to you. Lump charcoal can burn hotter, produce cleaner smoke, and generate less ash. Briquettes, however, burn more consistently and provide an even, predictable heat, especially if you stick with the same brand. Avoid self-lighting charcoal briquettes.

For this book, it doesn't matter which type of charcoal you use.

Other Kinds of Grills

The recipes in this book have been written for the average grill, specifically the gas and charcoal grills commonly used today in the United States. This includes kamado grills, of which we are big fans. (These are ceramic charcoal grills that have great insulation and an oval shape that regulates airflow.)

There are, however, other types of grills available, most notably pellet grills. You can make the recipes in this book using a pellet grill, but you may find that many models may not be able to reach the same high temperatures as a gas or charcoal grill. In that case, you may need to modify the recipes accordingly.

Electric grills have also become more popular recently, particularly with apartment and condo dwellers for whom full-size grills may not be allowed or practical. Electric grills are usually small and may not accommodate the larger items in this book. Most of our recipes will work, however. If you have an electric grill, stick to smaller food items with shorter cook times.

Similarly, there is a whole world of small, charcoal-powered grills that are fun to use but that may not accommodate indirect or dual-zone cooking. These include many portable charcoal grills and hibachi-style grills that do not have lids.

As we have said, many recipes in this book require indirect cooking or longer cook times at low temperatures. For your grill to produce these items properly, your grill needs a lid. If your grill does not have a lid, you will still be able to make any recipes that call for direct, high-temperature cooking. (Each recipe in this book has a tag at the top that tells you what style of cooking is required.)

Grill Tools

To do a job right, you need the right tools. Stores that sell grills are typically also overloaded with grill tools and accessories. Many of these accessories are things you don't need. That said, the proper grilling tool kit does require certain items. Most of these items can be purchased for a reasonable price, and you don't need the best of each tool, just tools that work. Keep your grill tools clean and indoors—except when you are cooking—and never leave them hanging on the side of your grill.

Spatula: We recommend a long-handle spatula that keeps your hands away from the fire. Options sold as grill spatulas are generally not great. They tend to be heavy and are more likely to push food around the grill than to flip it. We use a stainless-steel spatula from a restaurant supply store that is strong and lightweight.

Tongs: The same goes for tongs. Barbecue tongs are generally a waste of money, but sturdy clamshell tongs are perfect. Barbecue tongs are stiff and awkward. Look for lightweight, spring-loaded clamshell tongs that are around 14 inches in length.

Instant-read meat thermometer: Never trust the safety of your friends and family to your ability to judge the doneness of food by look and feel. When it comes to grilling meat, you can only judge whether something is fully cooked with cold, hard facts—which means using a reliable instant-read thermometer.

You can find these for under $20 or spend well over $100. The biggest difference between the expensive thermometers and the more affordable versions is the amount of time it takes them to read the food temperatures. If you want a fast read, you'll need to spend more money. Make sure to keep batteries for your thermometer close at hand, because they always die at the worst possible time.

Charcoal chimney: As we've discussed, if you use a charcoal grill, you need a way to light that charcoal outside the grill. A charcoal chimney lights coals quickly and easily and is a must.

Grill cleaning tool: Cleaning tools that use wire bristles are not great, as the bristles often break off and can get into your food. Instead, buy and use any alternatives that you can find online, ranging from the Brushtech Double Helix Bristle Free BBQ Brush to pumice stone cleaners like those from Earth Stone. Simply search for "grill brush alternatives," and you will find the right tool for you. We like the wooden grate cleaners from Grate Scrape.

Heat-resistant gloves: Sometimes, you will have to put your hands on hot stuff. There are several great brands of food-safe, heat-resistant gloves out there. These are the perfect tool for lifting whole chickens or large roasts off your grill without dropping them. We also recommend leather welder's gloves for handling hot metal items such as skillets, skewers, and rotisserie rods.

Aluminum foil: Foil is indispensable for many grilling applications. It can be used for packet cooking, wrapping foods for steaming or to hold them at temperature, and as a covering when resting meats before serving. Keep a large roll of heavy-duty aluminum foil on hand. We suggest several uses throughout this book.

Kitchen twine: Trussing and tying whole poultry or roasts is a must for many recipes. You can find kitchen twine in most grocery stores.

Rotisserie kit: We love rotisserie cooking; we even wrote a whole book on it! We always recommend a rotisserie kit for every grill, and that includes charcoal grills. There are some "universal" rotisserie kits on the market, but we recommend buying the unit specific for your grill.

Grilling planks: These thin wooden planks are perfect for grilling small or delicate foods such as fish or vegetables. You place the food on the plank, and the plank goes on the grill. As the wood heats up, it releases smoke and adds a whole new level of flavor to your dish.

Wire cooling rack: A wire cooling rack—the kind you'd normally use for baked items like cookies—is the perfect grill accessory. They are easy to find, inexpensive, and make grilling small items easy.

The Griller's Kitchen

Most recipes in this book use ingredients you can find in almost any grocery store. If you're planning to do a lot of grilling, there are a few items that you should stock up on, because they show up regularly in many types of grilling and barbecue recipes. This list will get you started.

Kosher salt: We are not terribly picky when it comes to salt, but we prefer coarse salt over common table salt. Coarse salt flavors foods slower but more completely and works best in pretty much every application.

Black pepper: Pepper shows up in most grilling recipes. Fine-ground black pepper is perfect for many recipes, but we like a coarse grind on the surface of meats to let that pepper flavor pop. Keep an adjustable pepper grinder handy so you can achieve the coarseness you prefer.

Paprika: Paprika gives grilled and smoked foods a subtle flavor and a powerful color. We use it frequently for the deep, rich red hue it lends to foods.

Apple cider vinegar: This vinegar has great flavor. We like apple cider vinegar because it adds a tangy pop to marinades and sauces. The apple gives more depth of flavor to grilled and smoked foods.

Apple juice: Although any fruit juice will add sweetness and moisture to a recipe, apple juice has a subtle flavor that nearly disappears when it's cooked. We use it when wrapping meats to add a little extra moisture (in the case of meats that might dry out before they're done cooking), in sauces, and for spritzing.

Broth: Adding a little broth is the perfect way to add a splash of moisture to grilled and smoked foods while maintaining the flavor profile. Match the broth to the protein: Use beef broth for beef dishes, for instance.

Garlic powder: What doesn't benefit from a little garlic? We use garlic powder in rubs and sauces because it is easy and blends in quickly. We do not use flavored salts, like garlic salt, because we want complete control of the amount of salt we use and when it is applied.

Onion powder: Like garlic powder, onion powder is a quick way to add a little flavor to any dish.

Cayenne pepper: We use a number of methods to add spice to our dishes, but when we're making fine adjustments to a recipe, a pinch of cayenne goes a long way.

Dried herbs: Fresh herbs are great, and we keep a number of them on hand, but dried herbs are packed with flavor. They also work wonderfully for high-temperature cooking, because fresh herbs will burn quickly and dried herbs retain their flavor as they cook.

5 IDEAS FOR BACKYARD BARBECUES

KC Barbecue
Kansas City Ribs (page 80)
Corn Bread in a Skillet (page 149)
Grilled Corn "Ribs" (page 136)
Assorted pickles

Healthy Cookout
Lemon-Rosemary Chicken (page 33)
Endive Caesar Salad (page 148)
Grilled Sweet Potatoes (page 141)

Mediterranean Night
Tuscan Halibut Fillets (page 122)
Eggplant Caprese (page 138)
Grilled Figs (page 152)
Pasta with olive oil and Parmesan cheese

Brazilian Barbecue
Picanha (page 90)
Baby Potato Kebabs (page 146)
Board Sauce (page 164)
Garlic bread

Steak House Burgers
Steak House Blue Cheese Burgers (page 98)
Grilled Corn with Spiced Butter (page 145)
Blueberry Cheesecake Crumble Dip (page 153)
Steak-cut french fries

CHAPTER TWO

Grilling Techniques

Grilling presents nearly endless cooking possibilities. With the right accessories, you can grill almost any food item. The secret is knowing how to set up and manage your fire. There are three main methods of grilling—direct, indirect, and dual-zone cooking—and each has a different setup for the fire. Pick the right one, and you can sear a steak, roast a chicken, or bake a cake.

So, don't simply turn your grill to high heat. Instead, learn how to master low-, medium-, and high-heat cooking and when to use each. That said, even the most advanced gas grill is not precisely controlled like an oven. Temperatures will be approximate, and the thermometer on the hood should be considered nothing more than a guide.

Direct Heat

Direct heat is exactly what it sounds like: Food is cooked directly over the fire. It is the purest form of grilling and what most people envision when they think about grills. It's how you sear a steak or grill vegetables. Direct-fire grilling is quick and easy, but it doesn't mean you're always using the highest temperature. Many delicate items, such as fish, fruit, and vegetables, are cooked with direct heat but need lower temperatures than burgers and chops.

The possible temperature ranges for direct-heat grilling go from a low temperature of 200°F to as high as 600°F. Some charcoal grills can even reach well over 700°F, but there is no reason to grill at a temperature higher than 600°F, and even that is just used for a quick sear. At this temperature, the surface of a steak will cook before the middle even gets warm.

What we like about high-temperature direct grilling is that it produces caramelization on the surface of foods. This is the flavor we associate with a properly cooked steak or burger patty. But remember, when cooking at these temperatures, you have to keep a close eye on your food to prevent it from burning.

How to Set Up for Gas

Direct grilling on a gas grill is easy. Light the burners, let the grill heat up, and you are ready to go. Once your grill is heated, turn the dial and adjust the heat to your desired level. It is easy to adjust the heat with a gas grill, and it responds quickly. We talked about the convenience of a gas grill in chapter 1, and this is where this style of grill shines.

If you have a large gas grill, you do not need to use all the main burners. The heated area of the grill only needs to exceed the size of the food you are cooking by 2 to 3 inches. Beyond that, you are simply wasting fuel if you turn on additional burners. Remember that direct grilling is about immediate heat and not the heat held inside the grill with the lid closed. In fact, with a good-quality grill and a thin cut of meat, you can leave the lid up while cooking.

How to Set Up for Charcoal

There are two ways to control the temperature in a charcoal grill. The first is by adjusting the vents. This limits or increases the amount of oxygen reaching the fire and slows it down or heats it up. The second way to control the heat is by the size of the fire. A bigger fire means more heat. Combining these two strategies will let you build your fire so it's either hot and fast or low and slow—or somewhere in between.

First, decide whether you need a high or low temperature for direct grilling. Second, decide how long you want that fire to burn. Grilling thin steaks? You'll want a searing hot fire for a short time. To build this fire, use a moderate amount of charcoal. Make a thick layer of coals in the center of the grill, larger than the area needed for grilling. Once the coals are burning and leveled out, put the lid on and keep the vents wide open to let the grill come up to temperature. Once your grill is hot, it is ready for those steaks.

A low fire may need a single layer of burning coals, spread out across the grill, with the vents partially closed to hold the desired temperature. Remember to use the bottom vent for fine adjustments.

Recipes to Hone Your Chops

Direct-fire grilling is perfect for thin cuts of meat or small items that cook quickly. It is also perfect for vegetables if the fire is adjusted to a lower heat. Try your hand with these recipes that use the direct-fire method:

Grilled Thai-Style Chicken Thighs (page 41): Chicken thighs can cook fast—and they can burn just as fast. This recipe uses medium-high heat to cook the thighs and lock in the flavors without burning them. As with all direct-grilled foods, the chicken needs to be turned regularly for even cooking.

Jumbo Shrimp Skewers (page 130): Getting shrimp cooked well requires high, direct heat and good timing. Shrimp can go from perfect to rubbery quickly. These skewers benefit from a touch of smoke, so we love to cook them on a charcoal grill.

Cauliflower Steaks (page 139): Grill these as you would a steak. Here, the direct heat roasts the surface of the cauliflower and locks in the flavors. This recipe calls for medium heat.

Indirect Heat

Indirect heat is the opposite of direct heat. This cooking method is much more like baking in your oven. In this case, you build a fire away from the food. This fire heats the air inside the grill, which is why you need to keep the lid closed as much as possible. With indirect grilling, you roast or bake instead of searing.

This cooking method is used for large food items, such as whole chickens, roasts, or casseroles. Indirect heat can also be used for warming food. It may be necessary to rotate foods for even cooking but, in general, you don't need to interact with the food as much as you do with direct grilling.

You can use this grilling method if you plan on low-and-slow cooking or are using your grill to make traditional smoked barbecue. You can even add hardwood to the grill and smoke foods easily while cooking them at very low temperatures. There are several configurations for indirect grilling, and they depend on the size and the type of grill.

How to Set Up for Gas

The best strategy for indirect grilling on a gas grill is to have the fire on both sides of the food. If your grill is large enough, turn on the end burners and place the food in the middle. Doing this surrounds the food with heat and allows for even cooking.

The two-sided configuration might not, however, be possible on a smaller grill, particularly a two-burner unit. In this case, light the heat source that is on one side of the food, and rotate the food several times as it cooks. The higher the cooking temperature, the more frequently the food needs to be rotated to prevent burning. As a general rule, the side of the food closest to the heat needs to be at least 3 inches from the fire, or that portion will cook too quickly.

When cooking with indirect heat, it's important to place a drip pan under the cooking grate. Otherwise, if you are cooking meat with a lot of fat, the drippings will accumulate on the flame tamers, and the next time you fire up the grill, all that grease will have to burn off. This could cause a spectacular flare-up.

How to Set Up for Charcoal

There are several ways to set up for indirect grilling with a charcoal grill, particularly if the grill has a large surface area. Many charcoal grills are round, which means you can build a fire surrounding the food, because, unlike the gas grill, a charcoal unit allows you to arrange the fire exactly where you need it.

Charcoal is a good fuel source, but it can be temperamental. A low-and-slow fire that burns for a long period requires plenty of coals held in check by a limited oxygen flow. But when you limit the airflow, it redirects to the hottest part of the fire. This might cause the fire to go out in other areas of your grill. The secret to making it all work is to get all the coals burning consistently and spread them to different areas, as needed.

The best strategy for an indirect fire with charcoal is to build a ring of heat that completely encircles the food. If you do this, you won't need to turn or rotate the food. That means you can leave the lid in place for longer periods and have complete control of the fire. One of the best ways to arrange this ring is to place a disposable aluminum foil pan on the coal grate to keep the coals in place—and, as a bonus, it will collect drippings.

Recipes to Hone Your Chops

Indirect grilling is used to make dishes such as barbecue ribs. It is also used to roast meat without burning it or drying it out. And it can provide the heat source to bake a loaf of bread or a casserole. Many of our recipes use this method because of its versatility. This includes:

Dry-Rubbed Chicken with White Barbecue Sauce (page 46): Here is a classic example of food cooked with indirect grilling. In this recipe, you spatchcock a whole chicken, season it, and place it on the grill. Surround the chicken with heat, and it won't need to be turned or rotated at any point in the cooking process.

Blueberry Cheesecake Crumble Dip (page 153): When baking on the grill, indirect heat prevents the bottom of your food from burning. This blueberry cheesecake dip requires low heat to melt the cream cheese gently and is a great example of how you can use your grill like an oven.

Brisket (page 106): Brisket is the hardest meat to cook in traditional barbecue. It needs a very long cook time at very low temperatures. Here, the indirect heat allows the meat to cook slowly enough to become tender and absorb flavor from the smoke.

LID: UP OR DOWN?

Should you leave the grill lid up or put it down? The answer is that you almost always want the lid down, unless you specifically want high, direct heat.

Putting the lid down holds the heat inside the grill, which increases the cooking temperature. If you are grilling indirectly or with a dual-zone fire (see page 23), always close the lid. This creates convection-style heat (where the heated air flows around the inside of the grill, cooking the food). However, there is a big difference between a gas and a charcoal grill when it comes to the lid.

For gas grills, the lid holds in heat. Although most gas grills are hot enough to do direct grilling with the lid up, a closed lid increases the cooking temperature dramatically. For most of our direct cooking recipes, the grill lid will be in the closed position.

For charcoal grills, the lid vent controls the fire and can hold the heat by limiting the amount of air reaching the burning coals. Take the lid off and air rushes into the fire, which spikes the temperature. On a charcoal grill, when using high, direct heat, grill with the lid off.

Dual-Zone Grilling

Dual-zone grilling means creating low- and high-temperature zones. It is best imagined as a two-burner gas grill with one burner turned to high and the other burner turned to low. In practice, this can look a lot like the setup for indirect cooking (especially on a gas grill), but you use the heat differently: You use a warm area for slower cooking and a hot area for searing.

There are several kinds of recipes that benefit from this type of fire. If you are doing a reverse-sear steak, for instance, you want part of the grill set to a low fire to do most of the cooking and a hot zone to sear the steak at the very end.

Dual-zone grilling is particularly useful on charcoal grills where you cannot easily reconfigure a fire while cooking. On a gas grill, however, you might not need this setup for a reverse sear, because you can turn the burners higher or lower, as needed, for each cooking step. Instead, you'd use this setup to cook two kinds of foods simultaneously, at different temperatures, by cooking one food over direct heat and another on the lower side of the grill. For instance, you could put a whole chicken on the indirect side (away from the heat) and burger patties directly over the flames or coals.

How to Set Up for Gas

The setup for dual-zone cooking depends on the number of burners on your gas unit and the type of foods you are grilling. Generally, half of the burners will be set to low and the other half to high. If you are doing a reverse sear, start the food over the cooler section of the grill while the hotter section heats up. This allows you to switch to sear without waiting for the grill to heat up.

Sometimes, if a recipe calls for a low, direct heat, but the food would benefit from a higher roasting temperature, then we will recommend a dual-zone fire. The temperature inside the grill (lid down) will be high enough to roast, but we will still get some of that direct-flame flavor.

On a two-burner grill, you need to set one burner to high heat and the other to low heat. In this configuration, it may be necessary to rotate foods for even cooking. On a three-burner grill (or something even larger), you can set up this fire based on the area you need for high-temperature cooking. If you're going to sear or reverse sear your food, it may only be necessary to set a single burner to high.

How to Set Up for Charcoal

Setting up a charcoal grill for dual-zone grilling takes a little patience. The secret is making sure that all the charcoal is burning. The hottest part of the fire can draw oxygen away from cooler portions in a charcoal grill, snuffing the fire in that area. Start with enough charcoal for a single layer of coals over half the grill and a double layer over the other half. Now, pile all that charcoal together to get it lit evenly.

Once the charcoal is burning completely (glowing and partially covered in white ash), spread out the charcoal. Bank (pile) at least two-thirds of the coals under one half of the grill area and spread the rest over the other half. The cooler side does not need a full layer of coals, just enough to provide a low, direct heat.

If the recipe calls for high-temperature searing, the hot side of the fire should have at least two layers of coals. For these recipes, you are creating a sear zone, which only needs to be large enough for the food you are searing; adjust this area as needed.

Recipes to Hone Your Chops

We use a dual-zone fire for a number of recipes in this book, but we don't always use it for the same reason. Sometimes we want a combination of high- and low-temperature cooking. Other times we want to have a lower direct flame and a higher roasting heat. These recipes illustrate these methods:

Reverse-Seared Tomahawk Steaks with Gremolata (page 94): This is a thick-cut steak, so it needs a slow roasting to cook through the middle before it gets an intense sear to give it that perfect crusty surface. Start this over low heat until the meat is nearly cooked through, then move it to intense heat for 60 to 90 seconds per side.

Lemon-Rosemary Chicken (page 33): Chicken leg quarters must be cooked through the middle to a food-safe temperature for poultry (165°F). You can achieve this with a dual-zone fire by roasting the legs over low heat. These leg quarters are then placed over the hotter side of the grill to crisp the skin before serving.

Ultimate Rib Eye with Garlic-Rosemary Butter (page 93): A dual-zone fire roasts the steak over low temperature and the high temperature setting allows you to sear it to dark, golden brown right before serving. The crust is beautifully caramelized and a stark contrast to the pink medium-rare doneness inside.

BARBECUE AND SMOKING

Barbecue is a specific form of cooking items like brisket and pulled pork that require very long cook times, low temperatures, and smoke. The smoke does more than just flavor the food; it causes a chemical reaction in the proteins that creates specific flavors and textures.

Smoking is simply a process of cooking over a fire that produces smoke. This is a more general term than barbecue. Because smoke seeps into foods slowly, smoke cooking is generally done at temperatures well below those used for most grilled foods.

If you are serious about smoking and making barbecue, we recommend purchasing a smoker. They perform much better than most grills (although there *are* ways to make it work on a grill, with a few tricks). That said, adding smoky flavor to foods is not difficult on most grills. If you're using a charcoal grill, it's quite easy—the grill already has a fire that produces smoke. All you have to do is add some wood chunks to the fire from species of trees that produce a nice smoke flavor. We prefer large wood chunks over wood chips for smoke production, but you can use either. The wood will infuse fish, meats, side dishes, and vegetables with extra flavor.

Gas grills, however, are not great at holding on to smoke. The problem is that gas grills are designed to pump air through the cooking chamber, so the smoke exits quickly. The good news is that there are many accessories on the market for making smoke in any grill. Our preferred gadget is a wood pellet smoker tube. It is self-burning and uses easy-to-find wood pellets as fuel. However, be aware that your gas grill will not provide a strong smoke flavor for the barbecue recipes in this book.

More Techniques

Beyond the techniques we've discussed, there are a number of other cooking methods you can use your grill for. One of our favorites is rotisserie cooking. With a rotisserie kit for your grill, you can cook anything large without much effort. You can also smoke on a grill, especially if it's a charcoal grill. Both of these methods require some accessories, but nothing too expensive.

Rotisserie Cooking

Almost every grill manufacturer offers a rotisserie system for their grills—and some even come standard with the grill. We consider this the one must-have accessory. We know you are familiar with rotisserie chickens you find at your local grocery, but there are so many *other* things you can cook this way. Roast beef, for instance, is best cooked on a rotisserie.

Rotisserie grilling is a form of indirect grilling: You center the food on your rotisserie rod between the gas burners or piles of burning charcoal. What makes this cooking method so great is that anything you put on the rotisserie self-bastes. Juices run around the food as it turns, keeping food moister than when you cook it with indirect grilling.

The setup for rotisserie cooking is simple. A rotisserie kit comes with a rod, a pair of forks to hold the food in place, and an electric motor. We recommend putting an aluminum foil drip pan under the food to keep your grill clean, but aside from this, follow the manufacturer's instructions and check out our rotisserie grilling cookbook for 75 great recipes.

Smoking

Smoked foods have become extremely popular of late. There is a big difference between smoking on a charcoal grill and smoking on a gas grill. With a charcoal grill, all you need to do is set it up for indirect grilling at a low temperature (between 225° and 250°F) for several hours, then add wood chunks to the burning charcoal. Place the lid on the grill and let the food cook.

On a gas grill, this is more difficult. You can't simply place chunks of wood on your gas grill and expect to get any smoke. Also, a gas grill has a large amount of air flowing through it and there is no way to restrict this. The smoke you make inside a gas grill won't stay there. But you can still get a good, smoky flavor into your food. Plan on indirect grilling at a low temperature.

For smoke production, we like the A-Maze-N Tube smoking device. This is a metal, mesh tube that you load with wood pellets like those used in a pellet grill. You light the pellets on one end of the tube and place it inside the grill, near the food. As the pellets smolder and burn, they release smoke. A standard wood pellet tube can burn for up to 2 hours. For long smoking times you will need to refill the tube as it burns out, but these are easy to use and quite effective.

HOW TO CHECK FOR DONENESS

There is only one way to test for meat doneness properly: using an instant-read digital meat thermometer. You can buy a reliable one for under $20 and it will save you from having food that is overdone or, worse, undercooked. People will tell you they use other tricks for this, like comparing the density of the meat to the feeling of pushing on the heel of their thumb, but these methods do not always work and are imprecise. (All hands are not the same, and neither is all meat.)

When checking meat temperature, put the probe into the thickest part of the cut. You want to know that the whole cut is properly cooked, and the part farthest from the surface cooks the slowest. Test multiple locations, being careful to avoid any bones, which can give a false reading, to ensure your food is cooked through. When testing poultry (where the proper temperature is particularly important for food safety), check the deepest portion of the thigh and do it on both sides. Each recipe in this book specifies the recommended doneness temperature for that food.

When it comes to fruits or vegetables, the internal temperature isn't as important, because these items can be eaten raw. For these kinds of foods, look for the desired tenderness and for browning on the surface.

Troubleshooting

Grilling is easy, but there are a few problems most people encounter at some point. We have tried to address best grilling practices earlier in this chapter, but to help you deal with any unanticipated problems, here is a list of the most common issues you might encounter at the grill, along with the ways we deal with them:

Flare-ups: This experience is the bane of every griller: Everything is cooking smoothly, and flames suddenly burst through the cooking grates. This is much more common on gas grills than on charcoal, but it can happen any time enough grease falls into the grill to cause a fire. Rule one, don't panic. This is a grease fire. Dousing it with water will *not* solve the issue. The best strategy is to let the fire burn out on its own. Move the food away from the fire, either to another part of the grill or to a platter. Once the grease has burned off, you can resume grilling as normal. We recommend trimming excess fat from meats before grilling to reduce flare-ups.

Charcoal that takes a while to start: It is particularly important to plan ahead when cooking over charcoal. Charcoal may not light or come to temperature as fast as you'd like. Light your grill early. It should have time to reach your target cooking temperature and stay there for a few minutes (about 5 minutes) to make sure it will hold at that temperature.

Uneven heat: Some people expect their grills to have perfectly even heat. Unless you spend thousands of dollars, you will probably not get that. Uneven heat is typical in most gas grills and a fact of nature on a charcoal grill. Heat simply doesn't move through a grill the way it does in your oven. But if you are an attentive griller, you can catch when some items are cooking faster than others. Pay attention and know that you'll have to flip those burgers earlier than anticipated or shuffle them around the grill. Take food items off the grill as they reach their recommended internal temperatures, even if only half of what you are cooking is done. (You can always wrap food in aluminum foil to keep it warm.)

Running out of fuel: Yes, we have discussed this already, but it bears repeating. Keep extra fuel on hand at all times.

About the Recipes in This Book

The recipes in this book offer amazing meal options and guide you through each dish's grilling process. The chapters cover the major proteins, and there's also a chapter on side dishes and one on sauces, rubs, and marinades.

Master these easy-to-follow recipes, and you'll be ready to take on more complicated ones in no time. All of our recipes have been thoroughly tested and are based on our many years of experience with live-fire cooking. We hope you enjoy every single one and that they inspire you for future cookouts.

To simplify things, each recipe begins with a breakdown of the time required, so that you can plan accordingly. Most recipes also include helpful tips:

Change It Up gives you ways to modify a recipe with a different ingredient or a new flavor profile.

Grill Like a Pro gives you specific ideas to improve your grilling for that recipe—and beyond.

Flavor Boost gives techniques that ramp up taste (like a burst of heat or a new spice combination) and elevate the recipe to a whole new level.

Pair It With suggests sides or combinations of recipes that fit together nicely.

Poultry

Lemon-Rosemary Chicken, page 33

Grilled Chicken Cordon Bleu

When most of us think of chicken cordon bleu, we envision the classic stuffed, rolled, and breaded chicken breasts. In this recipe, we've translated those flavors into an open-face concept. The breasts are flattened, quickly marinated, grilled in just 12 minutes, then topped with ham and Swiss cheese and served with a creamy Dijon sauce. *Serves 4*

PREP TIME: 15 minutes GRILLING TIME: 15 minutes

4 (6-ounce) boneless, skinless chicken breasts (1½ pounds total)
⅓ cup Dijon mustard
¼ cup honey
1 tablespoon white vinegar

1½ teaspoons soy sauce
1 teaspoon Worcestershire sauce
8 deli ham slices
8 Swiss cheese slices
¾ cup mayonnaise
⅛ teaspoon salt

⅛ teaspoon freshly ground black pepper
2 tablespoons chopped fresh chives

TOOLS: Kitchen mallet or rolling pin

1. Place the chicken breasts between two pieces of plastic wrap. Using the blunt side of a kitchen mallet, flatten the chicken breasts to a uniform ½-inch thickness.

2. In a small bowl, whisk the mustard, honey, vinegar, soy sauce, and Worcestershire sauce until blended. Remove ¼ cup of the honey-mustard mixture and set aside. Scoop 1 tablespoon of the remaining mixture onto each chicken breast. Gently massage the mixture onto both sides.

3. Preheat the grill for direct cooking at 375°F, or medium-high heat.

4. Place the chicken on the grill, close the lid, and cook for 6 minutes. Turn the chicken and cook for 6 minutes more, until the breasts reach an internal temperature of 160° to 165°F.

5. Top each breast with 2 ham slices and 2 Swiss cheese slices. Close the grill lid and cook for 2 to 3 minutes, or until the cheese melts.

6. Add the mayonnaise, salt, and pepper to the reserved sauce and mix to combine. Garnish the chicken breasts with chives and serve with the sauce on the side.

Lemon-Rosemary Chicken

Lemon and rosemary work beautifully together, and when paired with chicken and live-fire cooking, the result is phenomenal. This recipe is perfect for a quick weeknight meal yet fancy enough for casual weekend gatherings. If you'd like a touch of smoke, add some fruitwood, such as apple or cherry, to the fire. *Serves 4*

PREP TIME: 10 minutes, plus 4 hours to marinate **GRILLING TIME:** 40 minutes

4 chicken leg-thigh quarters

⅔ cup Lemon and Rosemary Marinade (page 168)

1½ to 2 teaspoons salt

Lemon slices to garnish (optional)

Rosemary sprigs to garnish (optional)

TOOLS: Food-safe resealable bag

1. Place the chicken into a resealable bag. Pour the marinade over the meat. Release excess air from the bag, seal it, and gently massage the chicken until it is well coated with the marinade. Refrigerate the chicken for 4 hours.

2. Preheat the grill for dual-zone cooking at 275°F, or low heat, on one side, and 450°F, or high heat, on the other side

3. Remove the chicken from the marinade, season it with the salt, and place it on the lower-heat side of your dual-zone fire. Discard the marinade. Close the lid and cook the chicken for 30 to 40 minutes, flipping once, until it reaches an internal temperature of 160°F.

4. Transfer the chicken to the hotter part of the grill (along with the lemon slices and rosemary sprigs, if using) and sear it for about 2 minutes per side, or until golden brown. The final temperature needs to be above 165°F. Serve immediately.

   Grill Like a Pro: Although chicken breasts can be cooked to 165°F, we recommend cooking dark meat to 175°F. Although it is technically done at 165°F, dark meat is much more tender at a higher doneness temperature.

Smoked Chicken Breast

The first time we made smoked chicken breasts, we were pleasantly surprised at how easy, delicious, and tender they were. Lean meats, such as chicken breasts, benefit from a hint of smoke flavor. We recommend using alder, apple, or cherry wood for this recipe. *Serves 4*

PREP TIME: 15 minutes   GRILLING TIME: 1 hour

4 (6-ounce) boneless, skinless chicken breasts (1½ pounds total)

1½ tablespoons olive oil

3 tablespoons Magic Dust Rub (page 159) or Poultry Seasoning (page 157)

TOOLS: Apple, cherry, or alder wood and basting brush

1. Preheat the grill for indirect cooking at 250°F, or low heat. Add the wood about 5 minutes before the meat goes on the grill.

2. Brush the chicken breasts on both sides with the oil and season with the rub.

3. Place the chicken on the indirect grilling area, close the lid, and cook for 1 hour, until the internal temperature reaches 165°F. Check the chicken breasts halfway through cooking. (Remember, each grill works differently, so cooking times may vary.)

4. Remove the chicken from the grill and let rest for 5 to 10 minutes.

5. Slice the chicken into ½-inch-thick pieces and serve.

Pair It With: Kansas City–Style Barbecue Sauce (page 162) or Easy Red Chermoula (page 171) and Endive Caesar Salad (page 148).

Jerk Chicken Skewers

These Jamaican-inspired chicken skewers are rubbed with jerk seasoning rich in Caribbean flavors like allspice, cayenne, and cinnamon, then grilled hot and fast. The flavors are warming and lively. Before you begin, remember that jerk seasoning is moderately spicy, so adjust the amount of cayenne to suit your tastes. *Serves 6*

PREP TIME: 20 minutes **GRILLING TIME:** 15 minutes

2 pounds boneless, skinless chicken thighs	**1 teaspoon cayenne pepper**	**½ teaspoon ground allspice**
2 teaspoons onion powder	**½ teaspoon garlic powder**	**½ teaspoon ground cinnamon**
2 teaspoons sugar	**½ teaspoon freshly ground black pepper**	**2 to 3 tablespoons olive oil**
1½ teaspoons salt		**2 limes, quartered**
1 teaspoon dried thyme		

TOOLS: 6 to 8 wooden skewers, soaked in cold water for 20 minutes; and basting brush

1. Preheat the grill for direct cooking at 375° to 400°F, or medium-high heat.

2. Remove excess fat from the chicken and discard it. Cut the thighs into 1-inch cubes. Thread 5 or 6 chicken cubes onto each skewer. Do not over-crowd the meat.

3. In a small bowl, stir together the onion powder, sugar, salt, thyme, cayenne to taste, garlic powder, black pepper, allspice, and cinnamon.

4. Brush the chicken with the oil, then season both sides with the jerk rub.

5. Place the skewers on the grill, leave the lid open, and cook for 10 to 12 minutes, turning a few times during the process. Once the chicken reaches an internal temperature of 165°F, it is done. (Check each individually before removing them from the grill.)

6. Serve with the lime wedges for squeezing.

   Pair It With: This dish pairs well with a side salad or Cauliflower Steaks (page 139).

Chicken Suya

These wonderfully spicy, peanut-coated West African–style skewers have become popular globally in the last few years. Typically, this dish is made with strips of beef woven onto a skewer, but cooks have also used this flavorful mixture on seafood, lamb, and, of course, chicken. Our recipe follows a simple skewering pattern. *Serves 6*

PREP TIME: 30 minutes GRILLING TIME: 10 minutes

- 1 cup roasted unsalted peanuts
- 2 teaspoons cayenne pepper
- 2 teaspoons salt
- 2 teaspoons garlic powder
- 2 teaspoons onion powder
- 2 teaspoons freshly ground black pepper
- ½ teaspoon ground cinnamon
- 2½ pounds boneless, skinless chicken thighs
- 2 tablespoons olive oil
- ½ cup red onion slices

TOOLS: Food processor; 5 or 6 wooden skewers, soaked in cold water for 20 minutes; basting brush

1. In a food processor, pulse the peanuts several times until they have a meal-like consistency, then transfer to a small bowl. Stir in the cayenne to taste, salt, garlic powder, onion powder, black pepper, and cinnamon. Spread the mixture evenly onto a baking sheet.

2. Prepare the grill for direct cooking at 375° to 400°F, or medium-high heat. Cut the chicken thighs into 1½-inch cubes. Thread 5 chicken cubes onto each skewer and brush well with oil. Gently press each chicken skewer into the spicy peanut mixture, turning to coat all sides.

3. Place the skewers on the grill, leave the lid open, and cook for 5 minutes per side, until the internal temperature reaches 165° to 170°F.

4. Arrange the skewers on a clean platter and garnish with the red onion slices to serve.

    Change It Up: This recipe is often made with beef (tri-tip or sirloin steak) cut into thin slices.

Spicy Chicken Sandwiches

Forget those fast-food spicy chicken sandwiches. Our version isn't breaded or fried, but it's just as flavorful served with a delectable scallion sauce. We came up with the sauce when we found ourselves with an overabundance of scallions that we didn't want to waste. It was a hit and pairs well with most meats, especially chicken. These Spicy Chicken Sandwiches are perfect for weeknight meals, casual cookouts, and game nights. *Serves 4*

PREP TIME: 25 minutes GRILLING TIME: 15 minutes

For the patties
1½ pounds
   ground chicken
1 teaspoon onion powder
1 teaspoon freshly
   ground black pepper
1 teaspoon
   cayenne pepper

¾ teaspoon kosher salt
½ teaspoon chili powder
¼ teaspoon
   garlic powder
4 hamburger buns

For the sauce
¾ cup mayonnaise

1 large scallion,
   finely chopped
1 teaspoon distilled
   white vinegar
¼ teaspoon
   cayenne pepper
¼ teaspoon freshly
   ground black pepper

1. Preheat the grill for direct cooking at 375° to 400°F, or medium-high heat.

2. **To make the patties:** In a large bowl, mix the ground chicken, onion powder, black pepper, cayenne to taste, salt, chili powder, and garlic powder. Form the mixture into 4 equal-size patties. Place the patties on the grill, leave the lid open, and cook for 5 to 6 minutes per side, until they reach an internal temperature of 165°F. Remove the patties from the grill and tent them loosely with aluminum foil while you prepare the sauce.

3. **To make the sauce:** In a small bowl, stir together the mayonnaise, scallion, vinegar, cayenne to taste, and black pepper.

4. Assemble the sandwiches on the buns, placing a 1-tablespoon dollop of sauce atop each patty (or more, if you like), and enjoy.

> **Pair It With:** Double the sauce recipe and serve it as a dip for french fries.

Fire Wings

Hot wings, or Buffalo wings, are served all across North America in restaurants and bars. Typically, they are breaded, fried, then coated in a spicy vinegar-based sauce. Our version omits the breading and, instead of frying, we take these tasty morsels to the grill. Not only are they easy to make, but they also receive a double coating of the buttery, spicy fire sauce. Serve them alone or with a side of creamy ranch or blue cheese dressing. *Serves 6*

PREP TIME: 20 minutes **GRILLING TIME:** 45 minutes

2 pounds whole chicken wings

1 tablespoon olive oil

3 tablespoons Poultry Seasoning (page 157)

8 tablespoons (1 stick) unsalted butter

4 garlic cloves, minced

¾ cup Tabasco or other vinegar–based hot sauce

2 tablespoons distilled white vinegar

1½ teaspoons Worcestershire sauce

¼ teaspoon cayenne pepper

¼ teaspoon salt

3 scallions, white and green parts, finely chopped

1. Preheat the grill for direct cooking at 350°F, or medium heat.

2. In a large bowl, combine the wings and oil and toss to coat. Sprinkle the wings with the rub and toss to coat once more.

3. Place the wings on the grill, close the lid, and cook for 35 to 45 minutes, until the internal temperature reaches 175°F. Keep a close eye for flare-ups and adjust the grill temperature, as needed.

4. In a saucepan over medium-low heat, melt the butter. Stir in the garlic and cook for 1 minute, until fragrant. Add the Tabasco, vinegar, Worcestershire sauce, cayenne, and salt. Increase the heat to medium and bring the hot sauce to a simmer for 2 to 3 minutes. Remove the saucepan from the heat, cover, and set aside.

5. Once the wings are cooked, place them in a large bowl. Add the hot sauce. Using tongs, toss well to coat, then return the wings to the grill (reserve the bowl). Cook the wings for 4 to 5 minutes, until the hot sauce caramelizes. Transfer the wings into the bowl with any remaining sauce and toss again.

6. Garnish with the scallions to serve.

Bourbon Teriyaki Wings

Most of us are well acquainted with sweet, savory Japanese teriyaki sauce. Recently, cooks have experimented with different variations that include fruit, spicy chiles, or hard alcohol. We've found that the deep, rich flavor of bourbon pairs well with this sweet, viscous sauce. We especially love it on wings, where the bourbon provides a pleasant earthy undertone. *Serves 6*

PREP TIME: 15 minutes **GRILLING TIME:** 45 minutes

2 pounds chicken wings, flats and drumettes

½ teaspoon salt

½ teaspoon ground white pepper or freshly ground black pepper

1 cup low-sodium soy sauce

½ cup packed dark brown sugar

2 tablespoons rice wine vinegar

2 tablespoons bourbon

2 teaspoons Sriracha

2 teaspoons sesame oil

2 tablespoons cornstarch

2 tablespoons water

1 tablespoon toasted sesame seeds

1. Preheat the grill for indirect cooking at 350°F, or medium heat.

2. Season the chicken wings with the salt and white pepper. Place the wings on the indirect grilling area, close the lid, and cook for 30 minutes, until they reach an internal temperature of 165°F.

3. Move the wings to direct heat to let them crisp for 3 to 4 minutes. Keep a close eye on them so they do not burn. The internal temperature should be 175°F when they are done cooking. Transfer the wings to a large bowl.

4. In a medium saucepan over medium heat, bring the soy sauce, brown sugar, vinegar, bourbon, Sriracha, and sesame oil to a simmer and cook for 2 to 3 minutes.

5. In a small bowl, whisk the cornstarch and water to make a slurry. Increase the heat under the sauce to medium-high and whisk in the slurry. Cook for 1 to 2 minutes, until thickened. Pour the thickened sauce over the wings and toss to coat.

6. Garnish with the sesame seeds to serve.

Grilled Thai-Style Chicken Thighs

This must be our all-time favorite boneless chicken thigh recipe. If you are a fan of Thai curry, you will love the sweet, spicy, pungent flavors of this dish, with the bonus of a light charred flavor from the grill. We recommend using coconut sugar for the marinade, as it adds just the right bit of caramelized sweetness to the sauce. *Serves 6*

PREP TIME: 15 minutes, plus 2 to 4 hours to marinate **GRILLING TIME:** 10 minutes

2 pounds boneless, skinless chicken thighs

1¼ cups full-fat canned coconut milk

¼ cup freshly squeezed lime juice

3 tablespoons Asian-style red chili paste

6 garlic cloves, minced

2½ tablespoons coconut sugar or dark brown sugar

1 tablespoon kosher salt

1 teaspoon ground coriander

1 tablespoon vegetable oil

Handful fresh cilantro leaves

TOOLS: Basting brush

1. Trim excess fat from the chicken thighs. Place the chicken into a large, nonmetal bowl.

2. In a medium bowl, whisk the coconut milk, lime juice, chili paste, garlic, coconut sugar, salt, coriander, and oil to blend. Pour half of the coconut milk marinade over the chicken and toss to coat. Cover the bowl with plastic wrap and refrigerate for 2 to 4 hours. Set aside the remaining marinade.

3. Preheat the grill for direct cooking at 350°F, or medium heat.

4. In a saucepan over medium-high heat, bring the reserved marinade to a quick boil. Reduce the heat to medium-low and simmer for 3 to 4 minutes. Remove the basting sauce from heat, cover, and keep warm.

5. Remove the chicken from the marinade, discard the used marinade, and place the chicken on the grill. Leave the lid open and cook for 3 minutes. Flip the chicken and baste with the basting sauce. Repeat two or three more times, until the chicken has cooked to an internal temperature of 175°F.

6. Garnish the chicken with cilantro to serve.

Mustard Chicken

In this recipe, chicken legs and thighs are marinated in mustard and dark beer, then grilled. The flavor is slightly tart, deliciously savory, and reminiscent of the German-inspired foods at one of our favorite events, Oktoberfest. We recommend serving this chicken dish with sauerkraut and mashed potatoes for the full Oktoberfest experience. *Serves 6*

PREP TIME: 10 minutes, plus 6 to 12 hours to marinate **GRILLING TIME:** 45 minutes, plus 10 minutes to rest

1¼ cups dark lager

½ cup peanut oil, walnut oil, or vegetable oil

Juice of 2 lemons

1 tablespoon Dijon mustard

4 garlic cloves, minced

1½ teaspoons freshly ground black pepper

1½ teaspoons onion powder

½ teaspoon dried marjoram

6 chicken drumsticks

6 bone-in chicken thighs

1½ teaspoons salt

1. In a medium bowl, whisk the lager, oil, lemon juice, mustard, garlic, pepper, onion powder, and marjoram to blend.

2. Place the chicken drumsticks and thighs into a large, nonmetal bowl. Add the marinade and, using tongs, turn the chicken to coat. Cover the bowl with plastic wrap and refrigerate for 6 to 12 hours.

3. Preheat the grill for indirect cooking at 350°F, or medium heat.

4. Remove the chicken from the marinade, season it with salt, and place it on the indirect grilling area. Close the lid and cook for 45 minutes, until the chicken reaches an internal temperature of 175°F. Discard the marinade.

5. Remove the chicken from the grill, let stand for 5 to 10 minutes, and serve.

> **Grill Like a Pro:** Chicken breast is cooked at 165°F. We recommend cooking chicken thighs to an internal temperature of 175° to 180°F. At this temperature, the collagen breaks down, resulting in juicy, tender meat.

Old-School Barbecue Chicken

Kids who grew up in the 1970s, '80s, and '90s are well acquainted with this Old-School Barbecue Chicken. It was simple and delicious, and the best part was that each family had their signature barbecue sauce. Some folks added a little rum or whiskey to the sauce, and others spiced it up with hot sauce. Whatever magic our parents or grandparents worked, it was beautiful and, of course, memorable. *Serves 6*

PREP TIME: 25 minutes **GRILLING TIME:** 55 minutes

6 bone-in, skin-on chicken thighs	**1 tablespoon olive oil or walnut oil**	**1½ cups Maple-Whiskey Sauce (page 167)**
6 chicken drumsticks (legs)	**⅓ cup Poultry Seasoning (page 157)**	

TOOLS: Basting brush

1. Preheat the grill for indirect cooking at 350°F, or medium heat.

2. Trim the excess skin from the chicken thighs and drumsticks, leaving a small amount intact. Coat the chicken with oil and season well with the rub.

3. Place the chicken on the indirect grilling area, close the lid, and cook for 30 minutes. Flip the chicken and cook for about 20 minutes more, until the individual chicken pieces register an internal temperature of 160°F.

4. Brush the chicken with the maple-whiskey sauce every 15 minutes, until the internal temperature reaches 175°F.

5. If you'd like the sauce to caramelize, carefully move the chicken pieces to direct heat for a few minutes, keeping a close eye on them so they do not burn. Serve immediately.

> **Pair It With:** Serve this with Grilled Corn with Spiced Butter (page 145) and a cool potato salad.

Buffalo Chicken Dip

Who doesn't love Buffalo Chicken Dip? It's spicy, creamy, and cheesy. We cook the chicken breast on the grill first, then assemble the dip—then back to the grill everything goes to finish cooking. You can take this recipe up a notch by adding a little smoke to the fire, which pairs nicely with the spiciness of the Buffalo sauce. We recommend using cherry, apple, or alder wood for this recipe. For the best results, add it right before placing the dip onto the grill. Serve with baguettes, crackers, chips, or chopped vegetables. *Serves 6*

PREP TIME: 20 minutes **GRILLING TIME:** 45 minutes

2 (6-ounce) boneless, skinless chicken breasts (12 ounces total)
Salt
Freshly ground black pepper
1 (8-ounce) block cream cheese, at room temperature

1 cup Buffalo sauce
1 cup ranch dressing
1 cup shredded Cheddar cheese, divided
½ cup blue cheese crumbles
¼ teaspoon cayenne pepper (optional)

¼ teaspoon freshly ground black pepper
3 medium scallions, white and green parts, chopped, divided

TOOLS: 9 x 9-inch aluminum foil pan

1. Preheat the grill for direct cooking between 350° and 375°F, or medium to medium-high heat.

2. Season the chicken with salt and black pepper on both sides. Place the chicken on the grill, close the lid, and cook for 8 minutes. Flip the chicken and cook for 8 to 10 minutes more, until the internal temperature reaches 160°F.

3. Transfer the chicken from the grill to a clean platter. Leave the grill on.

4. In a medium bowl, stir together the cream cheese, Buffalo sauce, ranch dressing, ½ cup of Cheddar cheese, the blue cheese crumbles, cayenne (if using), black pepper, and two-thirds of the scallions.

5. Chop the chicken into small, bite-size chunks and stir them into the cream cheese mixture. Transfer the cheesy chicken mixture into a foil pan, level it, and top with the remaining ½ cup of Cheddar and the remaining scallions.

6. Place the pan on the grill, close the lid, and cook for 25 to 30 minutes. (Check on it halfway through cooking to determine if it needs less or more time.) The dip is done when the cheese has melted and the sides are bubbling.

7. Remove the dip from the grill and let it cool for a few minutes before digging in.

> **Change It Up:** If you'd like to amp up the smoke flavor, use chopped Smoked Chicken Breast (page 34) and skip to step 4.

Dry-Rubbed Chicken with White Barbecue Sauce

Seasoned with a classic barbecue rub, this is our version of the traditional barbecue chicken of northern Alabama. The bird is spatchcocked (meaning it's cut open down the back, so it lays flat), then slow-grilled, carved, and dipped in a white Alabama barbecue sauce right before serving. Please note that the sauce should be served slightly warm. The easiest way to do this is to pop it in the microwave for 30 to 45 seconds, then stir thoroughly before using. *Serves 4*

PREP TIME: 25 minutes **GRILLING TIME:** 1 hour 15 minutes, plus 15 minutes to rest

For the chicken

1 whole chicken (about 3 pounds)

¼ cup Magic Dust Rub (page 159)

For the Alabama barbecue sauce

2 cups mayonnaise

½ cup apple cider vinegar

2 tablespoons freshly squeezed lemon juice

2 teaspoons sugar

1½ teaspoons prepared horseradish

¼ teaspoon garlic powder

¼ teaspoon salt

¼ teaspoon freshly ground black pepper

¼ teaspoon cayenne pepper

TOOLS: Kitchen shears

1. Preheat the grill for indirect cooking at 300°F, or medium-low heat.

2. Remove the giblets from the chicken. Spatchcock the chicken: Turn the bird over, so the backbone faces up. Using sharp kitchen shears, cut along one side of the backbone, going from the chicken's tail up to the neck. Repeat the process on the other side, removing the backbone completely. Turn the chicken over, folding it open, and press down on the breast section until it lays flat.

3. Season the chicken with the rub, making sure to get some under the skin covering the breast meat. Slide a finger or two between the skin and the breast meat, making a pocket. Push the rub into this space and spread it over the breast meat and down to the leg.

4. Place the chicken, breast-side up, on the indirect grilling area. Close the lid and cook for about 1 hour 15 minutes, until the chicken reaches an internal temperature of 165°F in the breast and 175°F in the thighs.

5. Remove the chicken from the grill and tent it loosely with aluminum foil. Let the chicken rest for 10 to 15 minutes.

6. **To make the Alabama barbecue sauce:** In a small bowl, whisk the mayonnaise, vinegar, lemon juice, sugar, horseradish, garlic powder, salt, black pepper, and cayenne to taste until smooth.

7. Carve the chicken by removing the legs and thighs first, then the wings. Remove each breast and slice it.

8. Dip or drizzle the chicken in the sauce before serving. Serve the remaining sauce on the side.

> **Change It Up:** This chicken makes fantastic pulled chicken sandwiches. Remove the chicken meat from the bones, shred it, toss it with the barbecue sauce, and scoop the mixture into buns.

Gochujang Chicken

Gochujang is a spicy red pepper paste used in Korean cooking. Our recipe combines the heat in this paste with a little sweetness from a mix of lemon-lime soda and honey, which balances the gochujang's saltiness. Gochujang is available online and can be found in Asian markets and with other East Asian ingredients in many grocery stores. *Serves 4*

PREP TIME: 20 minutes, plus 4 to 6 hours to marinate GRILLING TIME: 1 hour 15 minutes, plus 10 minutes to rest

1 whole chicken (about 3 pounds)

½ cup lemon-lime soda

3 tablespoons honey or pure maple syrup

3 tablespoons gochujang paste

1½ teaspoons soy sauce

2 garlic cloves, minced

2 teaspoons grated peeled fresh ginger

2 teaspoons toasted sesame oil

2 scallions, white and green parts, chopped

2 limes, quartered

TOOLS: Kitchen shears and glass baking dish

1. Remove the giblets from the chicken. Spatchcock the chicken: Turn the bird over, so the backbone faces up. Using sharp kitchen shears, cut along one side of the backbone, going from the chicken's tail up to the neck. Repeat the process on the other side, removing the backbone completely. Turn the chicken over, folding it open, and press down on the breast section until it lays flat. Place it into a glass baking dish.

2. In a small bowl, whisk the soda, honey, gochujang, soy sauce, garlic, ginger, and sesame oil to form a loose seasoning paste. Slather the mixture onto the chicken, getting it under the breast skin. Cover the dish with plastic wrap and refrigerate for 4 to 6 hours.

3. Preheat the grill for indirect cooking at 300°F, or medium-low heat.

4. Place the marinated chicken, breast-side up, on the indirect grilling area. Close the lid and cook for 1 hour 5 minutes to 1 hour 15 minutes, until the chicken reaches an internal temperature of 165°F. Move the chicken to direct heat and sear it for a few minutes, rotating, as needed.

5. Remove the chicken from the grill, tent it loosely with aluminum foil, and let rest for 10 minutes.

6. Carve the chicken, garnish with the scallions, and serve with the lime wedges for squeezing.

> **Change It Up:** Gochujang has a remarkable flavor, but if you can't find it in your local store, you can substitute Sriracha, which will provide a similar heat with a different flavor profile.

Bacon-Wrapped Turkey Breasts

These turkey breasts are butterflied; filled with a delectable cranberry, mushroom, and pecan filling; rolled; and wrapped with bacon. This is the perfect meal for weekends and special occasions. *Serves 8*

PREP TIME: 20 minutes GRILLING TIME: 1 hour to 1 hour 30 minutes, plus 10 minutes to rest

- 2 (4-pound) boneless, skinless turkey breasts
- 1 cup finely chopped cremini mushrooms
- 1 Red Delicious, Gala, or Fuji apple, cored and chopped
- ½ cup chopped pecans
- ½ cup dried cranberries
- 1 tablespoon minced fresh sage
- ¼ teaspoon salt
- ¼ teaspoon freshly ground black pepper
- 1 pound maple bacon slices (see tip)

TOOLS: Kitchen mallet or rolling pin, kitchen twine or toothpicks, aluminum foil pan, and kitchen shears

1. Using a sharp knife, butterfly each turkey breast to open it out. Place each butterflied breast onto a large piece of plastic wrap and cover each with another piece of plastic. Using the blunt side of a kitchen mallet or a rolling pin, flatten the breasts to a uniform ½-inch thickness.

2. In a medium bowl, stir together the mushrooms, apple, pecans, cranberries, sage, salt, and pepper.

3. Remove the top layer of plastic from the turkey breasts. Scoop half of the filling onto each breast and spread it out, leaving about 1¼ inches of uncovered turkey around the perimeter. Use the plastic to help roll the turkey breasts up around the filling.

4. Wrap half the bacon slices around each breast, overlapping each slice a little. Using kitchen twine, tie the bacon-wrapped breast, or secure it with toothpicks.

5. Preheat the grill for indirect cooking at 325°F, or medium heat. Place a foil pan under the grates of the indirect grilling areas.

6. Place the turkey breast rolls on the indirect grilling area. Close the lid and cook for 1 hour to 1 hour 30 minutes, until the internal temperature reaches 165°F.

7. If, at the end of cooking, the bacon is not crispy enough, move the turkey over direct heat and sear for 2 minutes per side, rotating, as needed, for even cooking.

8. Remove the turkey breasts from the grill, tent them loosely with foil, and let rest for 10 minutes.

9. Using kitchen shears, carefully cut the twine. Slice the turkey breasts into 1-inch rounds to serve.

> **Change It Up:** Although maple bacon is preferred in this recipe, you can use any bacon, including turkey bacon.

Festival Turkey Legs

Inspired by those delicious turkey legs sold at amusement parks and Renaissance fairs, these drumsticks are smoky, tender, and delicious. They are brined for 24 hours, then seasoned and grilled. Remember to omit the salt from the rub! The brine provides enough salty flavor. *Serves 4*

PREP TIME: 20 minutes, plus 24 hours to brine GRILLING TIME: 2 hours 30 minutes, plus 15 minutes to rest

1 gallon water

1 cup kosher salt

½ cup packed dark brown sugar

1 tablespoon red pepper flakes

2 tablespoons garlic powder

1 tablespoon smoked paprika

1 orange, quartered

1 to 2 cups ice, optional

4 (1½- to 2-pound) turkey legs

¾ cup Magic Dust Rub (page 159), made without salt

1 cup Kansas City–Style Barbecue Sauce (page 162)

TOOLS: Wood of choice (optional) and basting brush

1. In a large stockpot over high heat, combine the water, salt, and brown sugar and bring to a boil. Remove from the heat, and stir in the red pepper flakes, garlic powder, paprika, and orange quarters. Let the mixture cool completely. Add 1 to 2 cups of ice, if needed, to cool the brine. Once cooled, submerge the turkey legs in the brine. Cover the stockpot and refrigerate for 24 hours.

2. Preheat the grill for indirect cooking at 275°F, or low heat. Add the wood about 5 minutes before the meat goes on the grill (if using).

3. Remove the turkey legs from the brine and use paper towels to blot off excess moisture. Season the turkey legs with the rub (remember not to use salt in the rub; the brine provides enough salt flavor). Discard the brine.

4. Place the turkey legs on the indirect grilling area, close the lid, and cook for 2 hours to 2 hours 30 minutes, until they reach an internal temperature of 175°F.

5. During the last 15 minutes of cooking, brush on the barbecue sauce and cook until the sauce caramelizes the surface of the turkey legs.

6. Remove the turkey legs from the grill, tent them loosely with aluminum foil, and let rest for 10 to 15 minutes before serving.

Dry-Brined Whole Turkey Breast

One of the easiest ways to hone your turkey grill craft is to start with a whole turkey breast. This recipe is particularly good for people who love white turkey meat. Dry brining is a great way to boost flavor and tenderness as the meat cooks. We recommend not using a turkey breast that has been packaged in a sodium solution, because the flavor will be too salty. Instead, look for fresh turkey breast that doesn't say "enhanced" on the label. *Serves 8*

PREP TIME: 20 minutes, plus 24 hours to brine **GRILLING TIME:** 2 hours 30 minutes, plus 20 minutes to rest

1 (9- to 10-pound) frozen
  bone-in turkey breast
3 tablespoons kosher salt
1½ teaspoons sugar

1 teaspoon dried
  rosemary
1 teaspoon dried sage
1 teaspoon dried
  marjoram

1 teaspoon garlic powder
½ cup Basting Sauce
  (page 165)

TOOLS: Large food-safe resealable bag, aluminum foil pan, apple or cherry wood (optional), and basting brush

1. Two to 2½ days before brining (and 3 days before cooking), thaw the frozen turkey breast in the refrigerator.

2. In a small bowl, stir together the salt, sugar, rosemary, sage, marjoram, and garlic powder. Rub the dry brine all over the turkey, making sure to get it under the skin of both breast halves. Place the turkey in a large resealable bag, then seal the bag, pushing out as much air as possible, and refrigerate for 24 hours.

3. Preheat the grill for indirect cooking at 350° to 375°F, or medium to medium-high heat. Add the wood about 5 minutes before the meat goes on the grill (if using). Place a foil pan under the grates of the indirect grilling area.

4. Remove the turkey from the refrigerator. Using paper towels, blot off excess moisture. Place the turkey, bone-side down, on the indirect grilling area and close the lid. Plan on about 15 minutes per pound, or 2 hours to 2 hours 30 minutes of total cooking time.

5. After the first hour, brush the turkey breast with the basting sauce every 30 minutes. Once the thickest part of the turkey breast reaches an internal temperature of 165°F, it is done.

6. Remove the turkey from the grill, tent it loosely with foil, and let rest for 20 minutes.

7. To carve, remove the breast sections, cut the meat into ½-inch-thick slices, and serve.

8. Refrigerate any leftovers in an airtight container for up to 4 days.

> **Grill Like a Pro:** Turn this into a smoked turkey breast by adding a smoke source to your grill (see chapter 2, page 26). Reduce the cooking temperature to 275°F and increase the cooking time to 4 to 5 hours.

Grilled Duck Breast with Orange Marmalade Sauce

Duck breast is quite easy to cook once you get the hang of it. This duck is seasoned simply and then seared to medium-rare in a cast-iron skillet on the grill. The skillet will hold and transfer the heat to the duck breasts, giving them an irresistible crispy surface. Once cooked, the breasts are sliced and topped with a deliciously sweet-and-savory orange marmalade sauce. It's important to pre-salt the duck breasts. *Serves 4*

PREP TIME: 15 minutes, plus 20 minutes to stand GRILLING TIME: 10 minutes

¼ cup orange marmalade

¼ cup freshly squeezed orange juice

2 teaspoons soy sauce

1 teaspoon Dijon mustard

⅛ teaspoon white pepper

4 (5- to 6-ounce) duck breasts (Pekin variety; 1¼ to 1½ pounds total)

1 teaspoon salt

2 teaspoons oil or duck fat (see tip)

TOOLS: Cherry wood (optional) and 12-inch cast-iron skillet

1. In a small saucepan over medium heat, combine the marmalade, orange juice, soy sauce, mustard, and white pepper. Cook, stirring occasionally, for 2 to 3 minutes. Once melted through and well-combined, remove the sauce from the heat, cover, and keep it warm.

2. Using a sharp knife, score the fatty skin side of the duck breasts (score only the fat, not the meat). Season both sides of the duck with salt. Let the breasts stand for 15 to 20 minutes while the grill heats.

3. Preheat the grill for direct cooking at 450°F, or high heat. Add the wood about 5 minutes before you put the meat on the grill (if using).

4. Once up to temperature, place the cast-iron skillet on the grill. Let it heat until a light smoke forms.

5. Use paper towels to blot off excess salt and moisture from the duck breasts. Place the breasts, skin-side down, in the hot skillet and cook for 3 to 4 minutes.

6. Add a little oil to the skillet and flip the breasts onto the meat side. Cook for 2 to 3 minutes, depending on your preferred doneness—for medium-rare to medium, aim for an internal temperature of between 135° and 145°F. (Note: The USDA recommends cooking duck to an internal temperature of 170°F.)

7. Remove the duck breasts from the grill, tent them loosely with aluminum foil, and let rest for 5 to 7 minutes.

8. Slice the duck breasts and serve topped with the marmalade sauce.

> **Grill Like a Pro:** When using oil on the grill or when doing high-temperature cooking, choose an oil with a high smoke point, such as canola or peanut oil.

CHAPTER FOUR

Pork

Kansas City Ribs, page 80

Garlic-Honey Pork Chops

These sweet and savory grilled boneless loin chops are easy to make but oh so delicious! Keep in mind that loin chops can dry out quickly as they cook, so keep an instant-read thermometer close by, so you can pull them from the grill at the right moment. *Serves 4*

PREP TIME: 15 minutes, plus 4 hours to marinate GRILLING TIME: 20 minutes

4 (1½-inch-thick)
   boneless pork
   loin chops
½ cup honey, warmed

¼ cup freshly squeezed
   lemon juice
3 tablespoons soy sauce
4 garlic cloves, minced
½ teaspoon salt

½ teaspoon freshly
   ground black pepper
1 tablespoon chopped
   fresh chives

TOOLS: Medium glass dish and basting brush

1. Place the pork chops into a medium glass dish.

2. In a small bowl, stir together the honey, lemon juice, soy sauce, and garlic. Pour half of the mixture over the chops and, using clean hands, massage it into both sides of the pork. Cover the dish with plastic wrap and refrigerate for 4 hours. Reserve the remaining mixture for basting.

3. Preheat the grill for direct cooking at 350°F, or medium heat.

4. Remove the chops from the marinade, discard the used marinade, use paper towels to blot off excess moisture, then season them with the salt and pepper.

5. Place the chops on the grill, leave the lid open, and cook for 8 minutes per side.

6. In the meantime, on the stovetop or in the microwave, heat the reserved marinade until it is warmed.

7. Once the internal temperature of the pork chops reaches 135°F, baste the chops with the warmed marinade every few minutes until they reach an internal temperature between 145°and 155°F (medium-rare to medium).

8. Garnish the pork chops with the chives to serve.

Kansas City–Style Pork Steaks

Pork steaks have grown immensely popular in the last few years. Not only are they inexpensive, but they also lend themselves to low-and-slow cooking. These pork steaks are brushed with Kansas City barbecue sauce as they finish cooking. *Serves 4*

PREP TIME: 15 minutes **GRILLING TIME:** 1 hour 30 minutes, plus 10 minutes to rest

⅓ cup packed dark brown sugar

1½ tablespoons chili powder

1½ tablespoons kosher salt

2 teaspoons freshly ground black pepper

1 teaspoon garlic powder

4 (½- to ¾-inch-thick) pork steaks

½ cup apple juice

1½ cups Kansas City–Style Barbecue Sauce (page 162)

TOOLS: Apple, pecan, or hickory wood (optional); spray bottle; and basting brush

1. Preheat the grill for indirect cooking at 275°F, or low heat. Add the wood about 5 minutes before the meat goes on the grill (if using).

2. In a small bowl, stir together the brown sugar, chili powder, salt, pepper, and garlic powder. Season the pork steaks well on both sides with the spice mixture.

3. Place the steaks on the indirect grilling area, close the lid, and cook for about 1½ hours, checking on the pork after 45 minutes.

4. Pour the apple juice into a spray bottle and spritz the pork steaks. Close the lid and continue cooking until the pork steaks reach an internal temperature of 170°F, then baste them with the barbecue sauce every 10 minutes until the internal temperature of the pork steaks reaches between 180° and 185°F.

5. Remove the pork from the grill and let rest for 10 minutes before serving.

> **Change It Up:** Apple juice is the most common spritz for barbecue and grilling, but there are many other great flavors you can use. We particularly love the brine from a pickle jar.

Vietnamese-Inspired Pork Burgers

These burgers are based on Vietnamese-style *bun cha*, pork meatballs. Typically, bun cha are served over rice noodles with chopped peanuts and assorted vegetables. Our version uses them as burger patties with equally great flavor but a slightly different packaging. *Serves 4*

PREP TIME: 20 minutes **GRILLING TIME:** 15 minutes

1½ pounds ground pork
4 garlic cloves, minced
1 tablespoon fish sauce
2 teaspoons sugar
2 teaspoons cornstarch
1½ teaspoons grated
  peeled fresh ginger

¼ teaspoon salt
6 scallions
4 hamburger buns
2 tablespoons
  vegetable oil
1 cup shredded lettuce

½ cup fresh mint
  leaves, washed
1 cup fresh cilantro
  leaves, washed

TOOLS: Basting brush

1. In a medium bowl, combine the ground pork, garlic, fish sauce, sugar, cornstarch, ginger, and salt.

2. Separate the scallions into white and green parts. Mince the white parts and add them to the pork mixture. Cut the green parts into long strips and set aside.

3. Using clean hands, mix the pork, then form the mixture into 4 equal-size burger patties.

4. Preheat the grill for direct cooking at 375°F, or medium-high heat.

5. Place the patties on the grill, leave the lid open, and cook for 6 to 7 minutes per side, or until they reach an internal temperature of 165°F.

6. During the last few minutes, brush the inside of the hamburger buns with the oil. Place the buns, oiled-side down, on the grill and toast for 1 to 2 minutes.

7. Remove the burgers and buns from the grill, assemble the sandwiches, and serve topped with the lettuce, reserved scallion, mint, and cilantro.

Smoky Bratwurst Burgers

If you need a quick and delicious meal for weeknights and impromptu gatherings, these sweet, smoky burgers will do the trick. The first time we made these, they were the hit of the party. The patties are infused with a little smoky flavor as they cook; we recommend using apple or maple wood. *Serves 4*

PREP TIME: 20 minutes GRILLING TIME: 15 minutes

1 to 1¼ pounds bratwurst
  sausages

2 teaspoons Magic
  Dust Rub (page 159),
  or your favorite
  store-bought rub

4 hamburger buns

2 tablespoons olive oil

½ sweet onion, sliced

½ cup Maple-Whiskey
  Sauce (page 167)

1 cup sauerkraut, drained

TOOLS: Apple or maple wood and basting brush

1. Remove and discard the casings from the bratwurst. Place the meat into a medium bowl and season with the rub. Using clean hands, mix the meat and rub, then form the meat mixture into 4 equal-size patties.

2. Preheat the grill for direct cooking at 350°F, or medium heat. Add the wood about 5 minutes before the burgers go on the grill.

3. Place the burgers on the grill, leave the lid open, and cook for 6 to 7 minutes per side, or until they reach an internal temperature of 165°F.

4. During the last few minutes of cooking, brush the insides of the hamburger buns with the oil. Place the buns, oiled-side down, on the grill, and toast for 1 to 2 minutes.

5. Remove the burgers and buns from the grill. Place the patties on the bottom half of the bun, top with onion, maple-whiskey sauce, the sauerkraut, and the top half of the bun.

    Change It Up: If you'd like more crunch in your burger, add some onion rings. Cook them in your oven or air fryer and use them instead of the sliced raw onion.

Cajun Breakfast Sausage

These flavorful sausages are great for breakfast and brunch. When making seasoned foods such as sausage, you will need to test the flavor before placing them on the grill (see step 2). *Serves 4*

PREP TIME: 20 minutes, plus 1 hour to chill GRILLING TIME: 10 minutes

1 pound ground pork

8 ounces ground breakfast sausage

3 tablespoons pure maple syrup

1½ teaspoons paprika

1½ teaspoons onion powder

1 teaspoon dried thyme

¼ to ½ teaspoon salt

½ teaspoon cayenne pepper

½ teaspoon freshly ground black pepper

½ teaspoon dried sage

½ teaspoon garlic powder

Oil or nonstick cooking spray, for testing the sausage

1. In a large bowl, mix the ground pork, breakfast sausage, maple syrup, paprika, onion powder, thyme, salt to taste, cayenne to taste, black pepper, sage, and garlic powder.

2. Test the sausage before you begin grilling: Heat a skillet on the stovetop over medium heat and add a little oil. Break off a small (1-inch) portion of the sausage mixture and cook it for about 1 minute per side, or until it reaches an internal temperature of 165°F. Let it cool and take a bite. Adjust any flavors as necessary.

3. Line a baking sheet with parchment paper.

4. Using clean hands, form the sausage mixture into 3½-inch-wide and 1¼-inch-thick patties and place them on the prepared baking sheet. Refrigerate for 1 hour.

5. Preheat the grill for direct cooking at 350°F, or medium heat.

6. Place the sausage patties on the grill, leave the lid open, and cook for 4 minutes per side, or until they reach an internal temperature of 165°F. Serve immediately.

Pork Belly Satay

Satay is a classic Southeast Asian dish of skewered meat grilled and served with peanut sauce. Traditionally, satay is made with beef or chicken, but it can be made with fish, mutton, or pork or with meat substitutes like tofu. We've taken this dish even further and used pork belly. This satay makes an excellent appetizer. The sauce will be popular with your guests, so you can double or triple it, as needed. *Serves 4*

PREP TIME: 25 minutes, plus 12 to 24 hours to marinate   **GRILLING TIME:** 25 minutes

1 (3-pound) slab pork belly, skin removed if present

¾ cup soy sauce, divided

1 tablespoon minced lemongrass, or 2 teaspoons grated lemon zest

3 tablespoons dark brown sugar, divided

2 teaspoons fish sauce

6 garlic cloves, minced, keeping 1 minced clove separate

2 teaspoons grated peeled fresh ginger

½ teaspoon freshly ground black pepper

½ cup smooth peanut butter

2 tablespoons water

1 teaspoon chili paste

½ teaspoon salt

TOOLS: 10 to 15 wooden skewers, soaked in cold water for 20 minutes

1. Cut the pork belly into 1-inch strips, then into equal-size cubes. Place the pieces into a resealable container.

2. In a small bowl, whisk ½ cup of soy sauce, the lemongrass, 2 tablespoons of brown sugar, the fish sauce, 5 minced garlic cloves, the ginger, and pepper to combine. Pour the marinade over the pork belly cubes, cover, and refrigerate for 12 to 24 hours.

3. In a medium bowl, whisk the peanut butter, remaining ¼ cup of soy sauce, the water, the remaining 1 tablespoon of brown sugar, the chili paste, and the remaining minced garlic clove to blend. For a smoother sauce, combine the ingredients in a blender and puree until smooth. Refrigerate the sauce in a sealed container until needed.

4. Preheat the grill for direct cooking at 350°F, or medium heat.

5. Remove the satay sauce from the refrigerator and let it come to room temperature.

6. Thread 6 pork belly cubes onto each skewer. Season the pork with the salt. Place the skewers on the grill, leave the lid open, and cook for 25 minutes, or until the pork cubes reach an internal temperature of 160°F, turning the skewers a few times while cooking.

7. Once the pork belly has crisped up and has a golden-brown color, serve with the satay sauce for dipping.

   Grill Like a Pro: Pork belly is delicious but quite rich. We recommend serving this satay as an appetizer. Remove the cooked pork belly from the skewers and arrange them on a platter with toothpicks and the satay sauce in the middle.

Grilled Ham Steaks

Nothing wakes up the flavor of ham steak like live-fire cooking—something about an open flame really intensifies the flavor. Add an orange-maple glaze, and these ham steaks are pure magic. They have an irresistible sweet and savory flavor that is perfect for any occasion. You can even serve these steaks for breakfast. *Serves 4*

PREP TIME: 10 minutes, plus 4 to 24 hours to marinate GRILLING TIME: 15 minutes

½ cup pure maple syrup
¼ cup freshly squeezed
   orange juice
1 tablespoon
   unsalted butter

1¼ teaspoons chopped
   fresh sage
¼ teaspoon cayenne
   pepper (optional)
Pinch salt

Pinch freshly ground
   black pepper
2 bone-in ham steaks

TOOLS: Basting brush

1. In a small saucepan over medium heat, combine the maple syrup, orange juice, butter, sage, cayenne (if using), salt, and black pepper and bring to a simmer. Once the mixture is well-combined and has thinned out, remove it from the heat, cover, and keep warm.

2. Preheat the grill for direct cooking at 350°F, or medium heat.

3. Place the ham steaks on the grill, leave the lid open, and cook for 5 to 6 minutes per side, depending on size and thickness.

4. During the last 3 to 4 minutes of cooking, brush the ham steaks with the glaze, flip them, and repeat. Serve immediately.

   Change It Up: Swap the orange-maple glaze for the Rib Candy Glaze (page 166).

Jalapeño Pig Shots

Pig shots make a great appetizer or game-day snack. If you're not familiar with these little gems, they're made of pork sausage rounds wrapped in
bacon and then topped with a jalapeño–cream cheese mixture. What could be
better? Nothing! *Serves 4*

PREP TIME: 30 minutes   GRILLING TIME: 1 hour 30 minutes, plus 10 minutes to rest

1 (8-ounce) block cream cheese, at room temperature

½ cup shredded pepper Jack or Cheddar cheese

2 medium jalapeño peppers, seeded and minced

2 tablespoons Magic Dust Rub (page 159)

2 medium scallions, white and green parts, minced

1 pound smoked pork kielbasa, cut in ½-inch-thick rounds

1 pound thick-cut bacon slices, halved widthwise

½ cup Kansas City–Style Barbecue Sauce (page 162)

TOOLS: Toothpicks and apple, cherry, or hickory wood

1. Preheat the grill for indirect cooking at 275°F, or low heat. Add the wood about 5 minutes before the pig shots go on the grill.

2. In a medium bowl, stir together the cream cheese, pepper Jack, jalapeños, rub, and scallions.

3. Wrap each sausage round with bacon, around the perimeter, securing it with a toothpick. It will look like a shot glass with the sausage acting as the bottom of the glass. Spoon some cream cheese mixture into each, filling to slightly below the top of the bacon.

4. Arrange the pig shots on a wire rack and place the rack on the indirect grilling area. Close the lid and cook for 45 minutes. Rotate the entire rack to ensure even cooking and cook for 45 minutes more, until the bacon is crispy and brown and the filling is puffed up.

5. Remove the pig shots from the grill, let them rest for 10 minutes, and serve with a dollop of barbecue sauce on top.

Char Siu Pork Tenderloin

Char siu is a Cantonese-style barbecued pork. The meat is coated in a flavorful hoisin-based sauce with distinct umami and sweet elements. Red food coloring is used to give it the traditional bright-red color. *Serves 4*

PREP TIME: 12 minutes, plus 2 to 4 hours to marinate **GRILLING TIME:** 40 minutes

- 2 (1-pound) pork tenderloins
- ¼ cup hoisin sauce
- ¼ cup honey
- 3 tablespoons soy sauce
- 3 tablespoons rice wine vinegar

- 3 garlic cloves, minced
- ½ teaspoon Chinese five-spice powder
- 1 teaspoon toasted sesame oil
- ¼ to ½ teaspoon red food coloring (optional)

- 3 scallions, white and green parts, chopped
- 2 tablespoons toasted sesame seeds

TOOLS: Food-safe resealable bag, aluminum foil pan, and basting brush

1. Place the pork tenderloins into a resealable bag.

2. In small bowl, whisk the hoisin, honey, soy sauce, vinegar, garlic, five-spice powder, sesame oil, and food coloring (if using) to blend. Pour half of the mixture into the bag. Massage the outside of the bag to distribute the marinade. Release the air from the bag, seal it, and refrigerate for 2 to 4 hours. Set the remaining sauce aside.

3. Remove the tenderloins from the refrigerator and let them sit at room temperature while the grill heats up.

4. Preheat the grill for indirect cooking at 250°F, or low heat. Place a foil pan under the grates of the indirect grilling area.

5. Remove the tenderloins from the bag and place them on the indirect grilling area, close the lid, and cook for 30 minutes, until the internal temperature reaches 130° to 135°F, turning as needed.

6. Baste the tenderloin with the reserved marinade and continue to cook the pork until the internal temperature reaches 145°F.

7. Remove the tenderloins from the grill and let them rest for 5 minutes.

8. Slice the tenderloins into ½-inch rounds and garnish with the scallions and sesame seeds to serve.

Adobo Pork Tenderloin

These pork tenderloins are marinated in a Filipino-inspired mixture of soy sauce, cider vinegar, and fresh garlic. The thing we love most about this recipe is its versatility. You can serve the first tenderloin as the main course one night, then chop up the second one and use it in hearty stews or soups. *Serves 4*

PREP TIME: 10 minutes, plus 4 to 24 hours to marinate **GRILLING TIME:** 20 minutes, plus 10 minutes to rest

2 (1-pound) pork tenderloins

¼ cup soy sauce

¼ cup apple cider vinegar

6 garlic cloves, minced

1 teaspoon onion powder

2 tablespoons olive oil

1¼ teaspoons kosher salt

½ teaspoon freshly ground black pepper

TOOLS: Food-safe resealable bag

1. Place the pork tenderloins into a resealable bag.

2. In a small bowl, whisk the soy sauce, vinegar, garlic, and onion powder to combine. Slowly whisk in the oil. Pour the soy sauce mixture into the bag. Massage the outside of the bag to distribute the marinade. Release the air from the bag, seal it, and refrigerate for 4 to 24 hours.

3. Preheat the grill for direct cooking at 350° to 375°F, or medium to medium-high heat.

4. Remove the tenderloins from the bag and season with the salt and pepper. Place the tenderloins on the grill, close the lid, and cook for 15 to 20 minutes, rotating every 5 minutes, until their internal temperature reaches 150° to 155°F. Watch for flare-ups and adjust the heat, as needed.

5. Remove the tenderloins from the grill, tent them loosely with aluminum foil, and let rest for 10 minutes.

6. Slice into ½-inch rounds to serve.

> **Change It Up:** Want more citrus flavor? Replace the marinade in this recipe with Mojo Marinade (page 169).

The Ultimate Pork Loin

This recipe uses multiple flavoring techniques all at once. The pork loin is brined in an apple and brown sugar mixture, seasoned with our Magic Dust Rub, then grilled to perfection—you can also add wood chips or chunks to the grill for a nice smoky flavor. Lean proteins such as pork loin tend to dry out during the cooking process. The brine combats that problem by plumping up the meat and keeping it moist and flavorful as it grills. *Serves 6 to 8*

PREP TIME: 20 minutes, plus 6 to 8 hours to brine GRILLING TIME: 1 hour 30 minutes, plus 15 minutes to rest

3 cups water	2 bay leaves	1 (3-pound) pork
3 cups apple juice	2 rosemary sprigs	loin roast
½ cup kosher salt	2 teaspoons black	¼ cup Magic Dust Rub
¼ cup packed dark	peppercorns	(page 159), made
brown sugar	1 cup ice, optional	without salt

TOOLS: Apple or cherry wood (optional)

1. In a large stockpot over medium-high heat, combine the water, apple juice, salt, and brown sugar and bring to a simmer, cooking until the salt and sugar dissolve. Add the bay leaves, rosemary, and peppercorns. Remove the stockpot from the heat and let the mixture cool completely. Add 1 cup of ice, if needed, to cool the brine.

2. Remove the silver skin from the pork loin. If it has a fat cap, leave it intact.

3. Place the pork loin roast into the cooled brine, cover the stockpot, and refrigerate for 6 to 8 hours. (Keep in mind that the brine solution must cover the pork completely. Use a bowl or large food-safe resealable bag, if needed.)

4. Remove the pork loin roast from the brine and use paper towels to blot it dry. Discard the brine.

5. Score the fat cap with a sharp knife, making sure not to penetrate the meat. Season the pork with the rub (made without salt).

6. Preheat the grill for indirect cooking at 350°F, or medium heat. Add the wood about 5 minutes before the meat goes on the grill (if using).

7. Place the pork loin roast on the indirect grilling area, close the lid, and cook for about 1 hour 30 minutes, or until the internal temperature at the thickest part of the loin reaches between 145° and 150°F.

8. Remove the roast from the grill, tent it loosely with aluminum foil, and let rest for 10 to 15 minutes.

9. Slice the roast into 1-inch-thick portions to serve.

> **Grill Like a Pro:** This pork loin roast makes great meat for sandwiches. It is, after all, the pork equivalent of roast beef.

Pork Rib Roast

Pork rib roast is a great replacement for prime rib. Not only is it a less-expensive option, but when grilled properly, it is also tender, juicy, and flavorful. If you're feeding a larger crowd, aim for a 10-bone roast and adjust your cooking time, as needed. This dish is roasted indirectly, then seared over direct heat right before coming off the grill. If you plan to brine the pork, omit the salt in the butter-herb rub so it doesn't become too salty. *Serves 10 to 12*

PREP TIME: 15 minutes **GRILLING TIME:** 1 hour 30 minutes to 2 hours, plus 15 minutes to rest

- 8 tablespoons (1 stick) unsalted butter, at room temperature
- 1 tablespoon fresh thyme leaves
- 1 tablespoon finely chopped fresh rosemary leaves
- 3 garlic cloves, minced
- 2 teaspoons kosher salt (optional)
- 1½ teaspoons freshly ground black pepper
- ¼ teaspoon ground cinnamon
- 1 (5- to 5½-pound) pork rib roast

TOOLS: Cherry, apple, or peach wood and aluminum foil pan

1. Preheat the grill for indirect cooking at 300°F, or medium-low heat. Add the wood about 5 minutes before the meat goes on the grill. Place a foil pan under the grates of the indirect grilling area.

2. In a small bowl, stir together the butter, thyme, rosemary, garlic, salt (omit if brining the roast), pepper, and cinnamon.

3. If the roast has a thick fat cap, trim it to a ¼-inch thickness, then score the fat in a crosshatch pattern. Using clean hands, slather the butter-herb rub evenly over the roast, avoiding the bones.

4. Place the pork rib roast on the indirect grilling area, close the lid, and cook for 1½ to 2 hours, or until it reaches an internal temperature of 145°F.

5. Move the roast to direct heat and sear it for 3 to 4 minutes to create a nice crust, rotating to achieve even searing.

6. Remove the roast from the grill, tent it loosely with aluminum foil, and let rest for 15 minutes.

7. Carve the roast between the bones to serve.

> **Grill Like a Pro:** When carving bone-in roasts or racks of ribs, stand the meat up with the bone side toward you. Slide the knife straight down between the bones for easy carving.

Pork Crown Roast with Fig Jam

Pork crown roasts are perfect for holidays and special occasions. Not only is the meat juicy and delicious, but these beautiful roasts make quite an impression. Crown roasts are made up of 2 racks of chops, tied together. If you are unfamiliar with the tying process, ask your butcher to do it for you. If you'd prefer to do it yourself, some great resources are available online. *Serves 4*

PREP TIME: 20 minutes, plus 3 to 4 hours to marinate **GRILLING TIME:** 2 hours 30 minutes

- ½ cup freshly squeezed orange juice
- 2 teaspoons grated orange zest
- 4 garlic cloves, minced
- 2 tablespoons olive oil
- 1 tablespoon chopped fresh sage
- 1 tablespoon chopped fresh rosemary leaves
- 1 bone-in, tied pork crown roast (10 to 12 bones)
- 1½ teaspoons kosher salt
- ½ teaspoon freshly ground black pepper
- 1 cup fig jam

TOOLS: Large glass dish or bowl, aluminum foil pan, and kitchen shears

1. In a small bowl, whisk the orange juice and zest, garlic, oil, sage, and rosemary to blend.

2. Place the crown roast into a large glass dish or deep bowl, bone-side up. Carefully pour the orange juice mixture over the roast. Using clean hands, work the marinade into all the cracks and crevices. Cover the roast tightly with plastic wrap and refrigerate it for 3 to 4 hours.

3. Preheat the grill for indirect cooking at 300°F, or medium-low heat. Place a foil pan under the grates of the indirect grilling area.

4. Remove the pork roast from the marinade, use paper towels to blot off excess moisture, then season it with the salt and pepper.

5. Place the crown roast, bone-side up, on the indirect grilling area, close the lid, and cook for 2 hours to 2 hours 30 minutes, or until the meat reaches an internal temperature of 155°F.

6. Remove the crown roast from the grill, tent it loosely with aluminum foil, and let rest for 10 to 15 minutes.

7. Meanwhile, in a small saucepan over medium heat, warm the fig jam. Once melted, remove it from the heat, cover, and keep warm.

8. For individual rib chops, use kitchen shears to cut the twine and carve the roast between the bones. Transfer the roast slices to a platter and serve with the warmed fig jam.

> **Pair It With:** Maple-Glazed Carrots (page 140) and Grilled Figs (page 152) make delicious accompaniments.

Grilled Country-Style Pork Ribs

Although this cut has been called country-style ribs for decades, they aren't actually ribs but, rather, strips cut from the shoulder region. This style of meat benefits greatly from low-temperature grilling to keep it tender and moist. If you'd like to add some smoke flavor, we recommend apple wood. *Serves 6 to 8*

PREP TIME: 15 minutes **GRILLING TIME:** 1 hour 30 minutes, plus 10 minutes to rest

3 pounds country-style pork ribs	¼ cup Magic Dust Rub (page 159)	1 cup Rib Candy Glaze (page 166)

TOOLS: Apple wood (optional) and basting brush

1. Preheat the grill for indirect cooking at 250°F, or low heat. Add the wood about 5 minutes before the meat goes on the grill (if using).

2. Season the ribs, front and back, with the rub.

3. Place the ribs on the indirect grilling area, close the lid, and cook for about 1 hour, flipping a few times while cooking.

4. After 1 hour, baste the ribs with the glaze every 15 minutes until the internal temperature of the ribs reaches between 145° and 150°F, about 30 minutes.

5. Remove the ribs from the grill, tent them loosely with aluminum foil, and let rest for 10 minutes before serving.

   Pair It With: Grilled Corn with Spiced Butter (page 145) or Bacon-Wrapped Green Bean Bundles (page 143) make this a mouth-watering meal.

Memphis-Style Spareribs

Memphis-style ribs are typically served "dry" (without sauce), but many people serve them with barbecue sauce on the side. These ribs are cooked using the "3-2-1" method: They are cooked for 3 hours, wrapped in foil for 2 hours, and then back onto the grill to finish up unwrapped for another hour. *Serves 4*

PREP TIME: 20 minutes **GRILLING TIME:** 6 hours, plus 10 minutes to rest

1 rack St. Louis–cut spareribs (1½ to 3 pounds)

1 tablespoon yellow mustard

3 tablespoons Magic Dust Rub (page 159), or 1 tablespoon per pound of meat

¼ cup apple cider vinegar

2 tablespoons butter

TOOLS: Hickory, maple, pecan, or oak wood and aluminum foil pan

1. Using a butter knife, remove the membrane from the bone side of the ribs; lift the membrane away from the bone on one end, then pull the rest away.

2. Apply a thin coating of the mustard onto the meat side of the rack of ribs. Season with the rub.

3. Preheat the grill for indirect cooking at 225°F, or low heat. Add the wood about 5 minutes before the meat goes on the grill. Place a foil pan under the grates of the indirect grilling area.

4. Place the rack of ribs, bone-side down, on the indirect grilling area, close the lid, and cook for 3 hours.

5. Remove the ribs and place them onto a large sheet of aluminum foil. Pour the vinegar around the sides of the ribs and top the ribs with the butter.

6. Wrap the ribs in the foil and place them back on the grill for 2 hours.

7. Carefully remove the ribs from the foil and place them, bone-side down, directly onto the grill grates. Cook for 1 hour more.

8. Remove the ribs from the grill and let rest for 10 minutes before cutting into individual ribs to serve.

Kansas City Ribs

Kansas City barbecue is known for its sweet, tangy, thick tomato-based barbecue sauce. The rub Kansas City cooks use is also quite sweet, with a rich brown sugar base that caramelizes during cooking. This recipe produces sticky ribs that are best eaten with a bib—or at least a pile of napkins close by. *Serves 4*

PREP TIME: 20 minutes GRILLING TIME: 6 hours, plus 10 minutes to rest

2 racks spareribs (about 3⅓ to 4 pounds each)
½ cup packed dark brown sugar, divided
2 tablespoons paprika
2 teaspoons chili powder
1½ teaspoons kosher salt

1½ teaspoons freshly ground black pepper
1 teaspoon onion powder
1 teaspoon garlic powder
½ teaspoon cayenne pepper
½ cup apple juice

4 tablespoons (½ stick) butter, cut into small pieces
2 cups Kansas City–Style Barbecue Sauce (page 162)

TOOLS: Hickory, apple, or maple wood; aluminum foil pan; and basting brush

1. Turn one rack of ribs over so the bone side faces up. Make a small cut at the top of the thin membrane over the bones. Grab the cut portion of the membrane with a paper towel and peel it off. Trim excess fat from the ribs and remove the folded end pieces. Repeat with the second rack.

2. In a small bowl, stir together ¼ cup of brown sugar, the paprika, chili powder, salt, black pepper, onion powder, garlic powder, and cayenne to taste. Season the racks, front and back, with the rub.

3. Preheat the grill for indirect cooking at 225°F, or low heat. Add the wood about 5 minutes before the racks go on the grill. Place a foil pan under the grates of the indirect grilling area.

4. Place the racks of ribs, bone-side down, on the indirect grilling area, close the lid, and cook for 3 hours. Keep an eye out for temperature fluctuations.

5. Remove the ribs from the grill and place each onto its own large sheet of aluminum foil. Pour the apple juice around the sides of each rib rack and top them with the remaining ¼ cup of brown sugar and the butter.

6. Wrap the ribs in the foil and place them back on the grill for 2 hours.

7. Carefully remove the ribs from the foil and place them, bone-side down, directly onto the grill grates. Cook for 1 hour more, basting with the barbecue sauce every 15 minutes until the ribs are done.

8. Remove the ribs from the grill and let rest for 10 minutes before cutting into individual ribs to serve.

> **Grill Like a Pro:** Sugar burns at 265°F. We cook these ribs low and slow, but remember, if you are using a sweet rub or sauce, keep the cooking temperature below the burning temperature of sugar or you risk ruining the food.

Pulled Pork

Pulled pork is very versatile. Pulled pork sandwiches are an all-time favorite, but we also use the meat in nachos, tacos, and more. Although the meat is traditionally cooked in a smoker, you can also use your gas or charcoal grill for the job. The secret, especially with a gas unit, is to keep smoke production going for at least 4 hours of the total cooking time, adding smoke materials every hour. *Serves 8*

PREP TIME: 20 minutes **GRILLING TIME:** 6 hours, plus 1 hour to rest

1 (4- to 4½-pound) pork butt

¼ cup packed brown sugar

2 tablespoons paprika

1 tablespoon kosher salt

2 teaspoons chili powder

2 teaspoons garlic powder

1½ teaspoons freshly ground black pepper

1 teaspoon ground cumin

½ teaspoon cayenne pepper

¼ teaspoon ground ginger

2 tablespoons mustard or Sriracha

8 hamburger buns

Kansas City–Style Barbecue Sauce (page 162) or your favorite bottled sauce, for serving

TOOLS: Apple, pecan, or alder wood; aluminum foil pan; and heat-resistant gloves

1. One hour before the pork goes onto the grill, remove it from the refrigerator, unwrap it, and place it onto a cutting board. Leave a ¼-inch layer of fat on the meat, but trim away any excess beyond that.

2. In a small bowl, stir together the brown sugar, paprika, salt, chili powder, garlic powder, black pepper, cumin, cayenne to taste, and ginger.

3. Coat the pork butt with a thin layer of mustard. Apply the brown sugar rub evenly to the pork.

4. Preheat the grill for indirect cooking at 225°F, or low heat. Add the wood about 5 minutes before the meat goes on the grill. Place a foil pan under the grates of the indirect grilling area.

5. Place the pork butt on the indirect grilling area and close the lid. Aside from when you need to add more wood to the fire, keep the lid closed as much as possible. Monitor the temperature of your grill during the cooking process. If using a gas grill, rotate the roast after 3 hours.

CONTINUED

6. After 3½ hours, check the internal temperature of the pork. If it has reached 170°F (if not, keep it on the grill until it does), wrap the roast in aluminum foil and place it back on the grill for 1 to 2 hours more.

7. After 5 to 6 hours of cooking, the internal temperature should be between 195° and 200°F. If using a gas grill and the pork hasn't reached 195°F, remove it from the grill, place it on a baking sheet, and finish cooking in a 300°F oven.

8. Once cooked, remove the roast from the grill (or oven) and let rest for 1 hour.

9. Unwrap the pork, pull the bone from the roast, and shred the meat by hand wearing heat-resistant gloves or use two forks.

10. Serve on the buns topped with barbecue sauce.

> **Change it Up:** For extra flavor and texture, top the pork with a slaw of 2 cups of thinly sliced cabbage; 1 jalapeño pepper, seeded and roughly chopped; 2 scallions, white and green parts, finely chopped; and ¼ cup of fresh cilantro. Mix the ingredients with a dressing made with ⅓ cup of plain whole milk yogurt, 1 tablespoon of apple cider vinegar, ½ teaspoon of sugar, ¼ teaspoon of kosher salt, and ¼ teaspoon of freshly ground black pepper.

Cider-Brined Pork Chops

Yes, pork and apples are made for each other, but this recipe takes the combination to a whole new level. Not only are the chops brined in apple cider, but they are also basted with a fantastic Maple-Whiskey Sauce toward the end of cooking. All these flavors marry well, resulting in a mouthwatering meal. *Serves 4*

PREP TIME: 20 minutes, plus 6 hours to brine **GRILLING TIME:** 16 minutes, plus 10 minutes to rest

4 cups apple cider
¼ cup kosher salt
¼ cup packed dark brown sugar

3 tablespoons freshly squeezed lemon juice
2 bay leaves
1 teaspoon black peppercorns

4 (1-inch-thick) pork rib chops
1 cup Maple-Whiskey Sauce (page 167)

TOOLS: Basting brush

1. In a medium saucepan over medium-high heat, combine the apple cider, salt, and brown sugar and bring to a simmer, cooking until the sugar and salt dissolve. Stir in the lemon juice, bay leaves, and peppercorns. Remove the brine from the heat and cool completely before using.

2. Place the pork chops into a large plastic container with a lid and add the cooled brine. Adjust the chops so they are submerged. Cover and refrigerate for 6 hours.

3. Preheat the grill for direct cooking at 375°F, or medium-high heat.

4. Remove the chops from the brine, lightly rinse them under cold water, and use paper towels to blot off excess moisture.

5. Place the chops on the grill, leave the lid open, and cook for 7 to 8 minutes per side, or until they reach an internal temperature of 150°F. During the last few minutes of cooking, brush the chops with the maple-whiskey sauce, flip them, and repeat.

6. Remove the chops from the grill, tent them loosely with aluminum foil, and let rest for 10 minutes before serving.

Beef and Lamb

Kalbi Ribs, page 101

Easy Mojo Steak Tips

Grilled steak tips—essentially steak cut into smaller pieces—have grown in popularity within the last few years. In this recipe, the meat is infused with a citrus-herb flavor from the Puerto Rican-inspired Mojo Marinade. Steak tips should not be confused with beef tips, which are small cubes of meat cooked in gravy. If you cannot locate flap steak to make the tips, use tri-tip steaks for this recipe instead. *Serves 4*

PREP TIME: 15 minutes, plus 3 to 4 hours to marinate GRILLING TIME: 10 minutes

2 pounds sirloin flap or tri-tip steak, cut into 2½-inch pieces

1½ cups Mojo Marinade (page 169)
1 teaspoon salt

½ teaspoon freshly ground black pepper
⅓ cup fresh cilantro leaves

TOOLS: Food-safe resealable bag

1. Place the steak pieces into a resealable bag. Pour the marinade into the bag and toss the steak with kitchen tongs to coat. Release the air from the bag, seal it, and refrigerate for 3 to 4 hours.

2. Remove the steak tips from the marinade, use paper towels to blot off excess moisture, then season the steak with salt and pepper. Discard the marinade.

3. Preheat the grill for direct cooking at 375°F, or medium-high heat.

4. Place the steak tips on the grill, leave the lid open, and cook for 3 to 4 minutes per side, depending on your desired doneness (we recommend an internal temperature of between 130° and 140°F for medium-rare to medium).

5. Garnish the steak tips with the cilantro to serve.

    Change It Up: If you'd like to add a more complex flavor to these grilled steak tips, season them with 1 tablespoon of Quick 'n' Easy Sazon (page 161) and 1 teaspoon of salt.

Carne Asada

Carne asada is a popular northern Mexican dish of marinated grilled meat, and it's the meat of choice for beef tacos. The name of the dish has become synonymous with an event, much like a barbecue, where close friends and family gather to enjoy each other's company and eat delicious grilled beef. Although this dish is wonderful for that kind of big gathering, we've found that it's also great for weeknight grilling, if you marinate it overnight. *Serves 4*

PREP TIME: 15 minutes, plus 8 to 24 hours to marinate **GRILLING TIME:** 10 minutes

¼ cup freshly squeezed lime juice

¼ cup freshly squeezed lemon juice

¼ cup vegetable oil

1 jalapeño pepper, seeded and coarsely chopped

3 garlic cloves, coarsely chopped

2 teaspoons ground cumin, plus more as needed

2 teaspoons chili powder, plus more as needed

1½ teaspoons kosher salt, plus more as needed

½ teaspoon freshly ground black pepper, plus more as needed

2 pounds skirt steak

TOOLS: Blender or food processor and food-safe resealable bag

1. In a blender or food processor, combine the lime juice, lemon juice, oil, jalapeño, garlic, cumin, chili powder, salt, and pepper and process until smooth. Taste the marinade and adjust the seasoning as you like.

2. Place the steak in a resealable bag and pour in the marinade. Massage the marinade into the meat, then seal the bag, pushing out as much air as possible, and refrigerate for 8 to 24 hours.

3. Prepare the grill for direct cooking or 450°F, or high heat.

4. Remove the steak from the bag and discard the marinade. Put the steak on the grill, leave the lid open, and cook for 3 to 4 minutes per side, until it reaches an internal temperature of between 130° and 135°F (medium-rare to medium) or your desired doneness.

5. Remove the steak from the grill and cut it at a 45-degree angle against the grain into ¼-inch-thick slices to serve.

Picanha

If you've dined at a Brazilian steak house, you'll remember the skewered picanha rump steaks that were sliced and served right at your table. The beauty of this dish is that you can make it on any grill, because the meat cooks quickly. When preparing these, don't cut off the buttery fat—it is the most prized part of picanha. You will need gaucho skewers or larger sword skewers for this recipe; these are available online and in specialty stores. *Serves 6*

PREP TIME: 15 minutes **GRILLING TIME:** 15 minutes

1 (3-pound) picanha roast	2 tablespoons Argentinian salt or kosher salt	Board Sauce or its chimichurri variation (page 164), for serving

TOOLS: 2 sword or gaucho skewers

1. Use paper towels to blot off excess moisture from the picanha roast. Trim off the silver skin covering the meat but leave the fat cap intact. Next, remove the small end pieces and cut with the grain into 6 (1¼-inch) steaks.

2. Form the steaks into a "C" shape, and thread 3 steaks onto each skewer. Season well with the salt.

3. Preheat the grill for direct cooking at 400°F, or medium-high heat.

4. Place the picanha skewers on the grill, leave the lid open, and cook 5 to 6 minutes per side for medium-rare doneness, or an internal temperature of 130°F. The fat cap should have a golden-brown caramelized appearance. Remove the picanha skewers from the grill and let rest for 10 minutes.

5. Carve and serve with the board sauce.

   Grill Like a Pro: If you do not have access to large skewers, you can cook picanha steaks like you would a New York strip (see The Lonestar Steak, page 107).

Fancy Filet Mignon

A filet mignon is simplicity matched with decadence. This cut is tender and deliciously beefy, and it lends itself well to simple seasoning. One of our favorite ways to prepare filet mignon is in a heated cast-iron pan on the grill, as it allows us to sear the filets evenly using intense heat. *Serves 4*

PREP TIME: 5 minutes, plus 30 minutes to stand GRILLING TIME: 15 minutes

4 (1½- to 2-inch-thick) filet mignon steaks	**1 teaspoon freshly ground black pepper**	**Board Sauce (page 164), for serving**
2 teaspoons kosher salt	**2 tablespoons olive oil**	

TOOLS: 12-inch cast-iron skillet

1. Season the steaks on all sides with the salt and pepper. Let the meat stand at room temperature for at least 15 to 30 minutes.

2. Preheat the grill for direct cooking at 450°F, or high heat.

3. Place a cast-iron skillet directly over the fire for 10 minutes, or until it begins to smoke, then pour in the oil.

4. Place the steaks into the hot skillet and cook for about 6 minutes per side, or until they reach an internal temperature of 130°F for medium-rare doneness. Remove the steaks from the skillet and let rest for 5 minutes.

5. Slice the steaks and serve topped with the board sauce.

> **Grill Like a Pro:** When you flip the steaks, place them on a fresh part of the skillet to maximize their contact with the hot cast iron. Because the mark of a great steak is its seared surface, you can take this recipe to the next level by buying filet mignons that are a cube shape (ask your butcher). When cooking, turn them onto each of the six sides for 2 minutes per side.

Ultimate Rib Eye with Garlic-Rosemary Butter

Cowboy-cut rib eye steaks are large, rather impressive-looking French-cut steaks that come from the rib section of the steer. These steaks are thick and contain a fair amount of marbling, much like what you find on a regular rib eye steak. If you cannot source a cowboy-cut rib eye, use a good-size rib eye instead and adjust the cooking time, as needed. *Serves 2*

PREP TIME: 15 minutes **GRILLING TIME:** 30 minutes, plus 10 minutes to rest

For the rib eye
2 (2-inch-thick) cowboy rib eye steaks
1½ tablespoons olive oil
2 to 3 tablespoons Central Texas Beef Rub (page 156)

For the garlic-rosemary butter
4 tablespoons (½ stick) unsalted butter, at room temperature
1 or 2 garlic cloves, minced

1½ teaspoons minced fresh rosemary leaves
1 teaspoon Worcestershire sauce
Kosher salt
Freshly ground black pepper

TOOLS: Basting brush

1. Brush the steaks on both sides with the oil, then season both sides with the rub. Let the meat stand at room temperature for 15 to 30 minutes.

2. Prepare your grill for dual-zone cooking at 275°F, or low heat, on one side, and 500°F, or high heat, on the other side.

3. Place the steaks on the low-heat side of the grill, close the lid, and cook for 10 minutes. Flip the steaks and cook for about 10 minutes more.

4. **To make the garlic-rosemary butter:** In a small bowl, use a fork to mash together the butter, garlic, rosemary, Worcestershire sauce, and salt and pepper to taste.

5. When the steaks reach an internal temperature of between 120° and 125°F, move them to the high-heat side of the grill, close the lid, and sear for 2 minutes per side to create a nice crust. Remove the steaks from the grill, top each with 2 tablespoons of the seasoned butter, and let rest for 7 to 10 minutes.

6. Serve whole or carved into ½-inch-thick strips.

Reverse-Seared Tomahawk Steaks with Gremolata

Tomahawk steaks are thick-cut rib eyes that have at least 4 to 5 inches of bone still attached to the eye of the meat. Butchers will French-cut these steaks for you, if you request it, removing all the fat and meat from the bones, so they resemble a slice taken from a pork rib roast or a rack of lamb. Because these steaks are thick, they are prime candidates for low-and-slow cooking. In this recipe, the tomahawks are slow-roasted on the grill, then reverse seared for a delicious crust. These hearty steaks are rested with butter and topped with gremolata, a flavorful lemon, garlic, and parsley mixture. *Serves 4*

PREP TIME: 20 minutes **GRILLING TIME:** 1 hour

For the steaks
2 (2-pound) tomahawk steaks
¼ cup Central Texas Beef Rub (page 156)

For the gremolata
1 cup packed fresh flat-leaf parsley
1 tablespoon grated lemon zest
2 to 3 tablespoons freshly squeezed lemon juice

2 garlic cloves, minced
¼ teaspoon kosher salt
¼ teaspoon freshly ground black pepper
½ cup olive oil
2 tablespoons unsalted butter

TOOLS: Food processor

1. Season the steaks with the rub 30 to 60 minutes before placing them on the grill.

2. Prepare your grill for dual-zone cooking at 275°F, or low heat, on one side, and 500°F, or high heat, on the other side.

3. Place the steaks on the low-heat side of the grill, close the lid, and cook for 45 to 60 minutes, or until the steaks reach an internal temperature of between 125° and 130°F.

4. **To make the gremolata:** In a food processor, combine the parsley, lemon zest and juice, garlic, salt, pepper, and oil and pulse a few times until the mixture has a rough-chop texture. Transfer the sauce to a small bowl, cover, and refrigerate.

5. Once the steaks are cooked to the right internal temperature, move them to the high-heat side and sear for 3 minutes per side to create a nice crust.

6. Remove the steaks from the grill, top each with 1 tablespoon of butter, and let rest for 10 minutes. While the steaks rest, remove the gremolata from the refrigerator, so it can come to room temperature.

7. Serve the steaks whole or sliced, topped with gremolata.

> **Grill Like a Pro:** You can infuse a little smoke into these giant steaks by adding cherry or pecan wood to the fire (if using a charcoal grill) or a smoker tube (if using a gas grill) a few minutes before putting the steaks on.

The Best Smash Burgers

Smash burgers are exactly what they sound like: smashed thin burger patties that cook quickly and are then topped with cheese and onion. Because of how thin they are, smash burgers are best made using a griddle on your grill or by using a flat-top grill. We love these burgers and make them for both casual gatherings and quick weekday meals. *Serves 6*

PREP TIME: 15 minutes, plus 1 hour to salt the onions **GRILLING TIME:** 15 minutes

2 medium yellow onions, thinly sliced	Freshly ground black pepper	6 American or Cheddar cheese slices
1¼ teaspoons kosher salt	2 tablespoons olive oil	6 hamburger buns
2 pounds ground beef		

TOOLS: Large griddle pan or flat-top grill and smash burger press or large metal spatula

1. Place the onions into a medium bowl, sprinkle with salt, and toss to coat. The salt will pull excess moisture from the onions, so they caramelize on the grill. Cover the bowl and refrigerate for 45 to 60 minutes.

2. Preheat the grill for direct cooking at 450°F, or high heat. Place a large griddle pan or skillet on the grill and let it heat up along with the grill. If using a flat-top grill, set it to medium-high to high heat.

3. Form the ground beef into 6 equal-size meatballs. Season them lightly with salt and pepper.

4. Remove the onions from the refrigerator and drain the excess water. Place the onions on a clean dish towel and wring out any remaining moisture. Transfer the onions to a clean plate.

5. Pour the oil onto the griddle or flat-top surface. Place 6 separate ¼-cup portions of onion onto the griddle and cook for 1 to 2 minutes.

6. Place one meatball on top of each onion portion. Place a small sheet of parchment paper over one meatball and smash it down with a smash burger press or large metal spatula to form a thin burger patty. Repeat the process with the remaining burgers.

7. Cook the burgers for 3 to 4 minutes, carefully flip them, and cook for 4 to 5 minutes more, until the internal temperature reaches 165°F. Top each burger with 1 slice of cheese during the last 2 minutes of cooking.

8. Serve the burgers on the buns with your favorite condiments.

> **Change It Up:** Try these smash burgers topped with cooked bacon or sautéed mushrooms.

Steak House Blue Cheese Burgers

These flavorful steak house burgers are inspired by "black and blue steaks" topped with blue cheese, barbecue sauce, and onion rings. If you can find blue cheese slices at your local market, they'll make it easier to assemble the burgers, but blue cheese crumbles work just fine. You can also use Swiss cheese or sharp Cheddar, if you prefer. *Serves 4*

PREP TIME: 20 minutes **GRILLING TIME:** 15 minutes

8 frozen onion rings
  (see tip)
2 pounds ground beef
1 tablespoon
  Worcestershire sauce
2 garlic cloves, minced

¾ teaspoon salt
½ teaspoon freshly
  ground black pepper
4 blue cheese slices,
  or ¾ cup blue cheese
  crumbles

4 hamburger buns
½ cup Kansas City–
  Style Barbecue
  Sauce (page 162) or
  store-bought barbecue
  sauce, warmed

1. Preheat the grill for direct cooking at 375°F, or medium-high heat.

2. While the grill heats, bake or air fry the onion rings according to the package instructions.

3. In a medium bowl, mix the ground beef, Worcestershire sauce, and garlic. Form the mixture into 4 equal-size patties, about ¾ inch thick, and season with the salt and pepper.

4. Place the burgers on the grill and cook for 6 minutes per side, or until they reach an internal temperature of 165°F.

5. Toward the end of cooking, place 1 blue cheese slice or 3 tablespoons of blue cheese crumbles onto each patty. Cook for about 2 minutes, until the cheese starts to melt.

6. Remove the patties from the grill and assemble your burgers on the buns. Each should have a patty first, then 2 tablespoons of warmed barbecue sauce, and 2 onion rings.

> **Grill Like a Pro:** We find that purchasing a bag of frozen onion rings from the store is handy for recipes like this one. Cook them in your oven or air fryer.

Smoked Meat Loaf

What better way to pay tribute to a childhood comfort food than to give it a modern makeover? Unlike the Sunday meat loaves of our youth, this recipe features two types of ground meat, as well as bacon, cheese, and barbecue sauce, all infused with smoke flavor. We recommend using pecan, cherry, apple, or alder wood for this recipe. *Serves 4 to 6*

PREP TIME: 15 minutes **GRILLING TIME:** 1 hour 30 minutes, plus 10 minutes to rest

1½ pounds ground beef
8 ounces ground pork
⅔ cup breadcrumbs
1 large egg, lightly beaten
½ yellow onion, diced
2 garlic cloves, minced

2 bacon slices, finely chopped
½ cup shredded sharp Cheddar cheese
½ teaspoon salt

½ teaspoon freshly ground black pepper
½ to ⅔ cup Kansas City–Style Barbecue Sauce (page 162)

TOOLS: 9 x 9-inch aluminum foil pan; pecan, cherry, apple, or alder wood; and basting brush

1. In a large bowl, mix the ground beef, ground pork, breadcrumbs, egg, onion, garlic, bacon, cheese, salt, and pepper. Place the meat mixture into a foil pan and form it into an evenly shaped loaf.

2. Preheat the grill for indirect cooking at 300°F, or medium heat. Add the wood about 5 minutes before the meat loaf goes on the grill.

3. Brush the barbecue sauce onto the meat loaf and place it onto the indirect grilling area, close the lid, and cook for 1 hour 30 minutes, or until the internal temperature reaches 165°F. (Check multiple spots for doneness.)

4. Remove the meat loaf from the grill and let rest for 10 minutes. Slice into 1¼-inch-thick slices to serve.

   Change It Up: Add 1 large jalapeño, minced, to the meat mixture to spice things up.

Pineapple-Marinated Tri-Tip Roast

Although tri-tip (a cut of meat popular on California's Central Coast) is usually cooked with a spice rub, we love to make it with Pineapple Marinade. The tropical fruit offers a slight bit of sweetness without overshadowing the meat's natural flavor. *Serves 4*

PREP TIME: 15 minutes, plus 4 to 8 hours to marinate and 30 minutes to rest
GRILLING TIME: 1 hour 30 minutes, plus 15 minutes to rest

2 (2-pound) tri-tip roasts
2¼ cups Pineapple
  Marinade (page 170)

2 teaspoons kosher salt
1 teaspoon freshly
  ground black pepper

TOOLS: 2 large food-safe resealable bags and apple or cherry wood (optional)

1. Place each tri-tip roast into its own resealable bag and pour half the marinade into each. Massage the marinade into the roasts, then seal the bags, pushing out as much air as possible, and refrigerate for 4 to 8 hours.

2. Remove the roasts from the bags, use paper towels to blot off excess marinade, then season with the salt and pepper. Let the tri-tips sit at room temperature for at least 30 minutes. Discard the marinade.

3. Preheat the grill for indirect cooking at 275°F, or low heat. Add the wood about 5 minutes before the meat goes on the grill (if using).

4. Place the roasts on the indirect grilling area, close the lid, and cook for about 1 hour 30 minutes, until they reach an internal temperature of between 130° and 135°F (medium-rare to medium) or your desired doneness.

5. Move the roasts to direct heat and sear them for 2 to 3 minutes per side, being careful not to burn them.

6. Remove the roasts from the grill, tent them loosely with aluminum foil, and let rest for 10 to 15 minutes.

7. To serve, cut the roasts in half, along the grain of the meat, then into ½-inch-thick slices against the grain.

Kalbi Ribs

This classic Korean dish uses flanken ribs, which are short ribs cut across the bone rather than between the bones. Traditionally, these are served, cut into individual pieces, with white rice, garlic, herbs (such as fresh basil, cilantro, and mint), and kimchi on the side, plus lettuce to wrap individual bites. *Serves 4*

PREP TIME: 15 minutes, plus 4 to 8 hours to marinate GRILLING TIME: 10 minutes

For the marinade
1½ cups soy sauce
¾ cup distilled
   white vinegar
¾ cup packed light
   brown sugar
2 tablespoons toasted
   sesame oil

4 or 5 garlic
   cloves, minced
1 tablespoon grated
   peeled fresh ginger
2 teaspoons freshly
   ground black pepper
6 scallions, white and
   green parts, finely
   chopped, divided

For the ribs
3 to 3½ pounds beef
   flanken ribs
1 tablespoon toasted
   sesame seeds
White rice, lettuce, herbs,
   and kimchi, for serving
   (optional)

TOOLS: Large food-safe resealable bag

1. **To make the marinade:** In a small bowl, whisk the soy sauce, vinegar, brown sugar, sesame oil, garlic, ginger, pepper, and two-thirds of the scallions until the sugar dissolves.

2. Place the ribs in a large resealable bag and pour in the marinade. Massage the marinade into the meat, then seal the bag, pushing out as much air as possible, and refrigerate for 4 to 8 hours.

3. Preheat the grill for direct cooking or 450°F, or high heat.

4. Remove the ribs from the bag and discard the marinade. Place the ribs on the grill and cook for 3 to 4 minutes per side until they reach an internal temperature of 145°F. Watch for burning and adjust the heat, as needed.

5. Garnish the ribs with the sesame seeds and remaining scallions, and serve with the rice, lettuce, herbs, or kimchi, if using.

Beef Back Ribs

Beef back ribs come from the rib section that is left over after the butcher removes the rib eye cap. These ribs contain less meat on the bones, as most of it is distributed between them. For this recipe, the beef back ribs are marinated, then seasoned with a dry rub before going on the grill. There is an optional saucing step, but trust us when we say that these ribs do fine without it. *Serves 6*

PREP TIME: 15 minutes, plus 4 to 6 hours to marinate GRILLING TIME: 4 hours, plus 30 minutes to rest

2 (3-pound) center-cut beef back rib racks

½ cup red wine

¼ cup olive oil

3 tablespoons dark brown sugar

2 tablespoons Worcestershire sauce

1 tablespoon soy sauce

2 to 3 tablespoons Central Texas Beef Rub (page 156)

2 cups Maple-Whiskey Sauce (page 167; optional)

TOOLS: Large food-safe resealable bag or glass baking dish, aluminum foil pan, and basting brush

1. Place the beef back ribs into a large resealable bag or glass baking dish.

2. In a small bowl, whisk the wine, oil, brown sugar, Worcestershire sauce, and soy sauce to blend. Pour the mixture onto the meat side of the ribs. Seal the bag or cover the dish and refrigerate for 4 to 6 hours.

3. Remove the ribs from the marinade at least 30 minutes before placing them on the grill. Use paper towels to blot off excess marinade, then season the ribs, front and back, with the rub. Discard the marinade.

4. Preheat the grill for indirect cooking at 275°F, or low heat. Place a foil pan under the grates of the indirect grilling area.

5. Place the ribs, bone-side down, on the indirect grilling area, close the lid, and cook for 1 hour 30 minutes to 2 hours, or until they reach an internal temperature of 165°F.

6. Wrap the ribs in foil or pink butcher paper and place them back on the grill, close the lid, and cook for 2 hours more, or until the internal temperature registers between 190°and 195°F.

7. If you'd like the ribs sauced, remove them from the grill, carefully unwrap them, place them back on the grill, and brush them with the maple-whiskey sauce. Close the lid and cook the ribs for 10 to 15 minutes.

8. Remove the ribs from the grill, tent them loosely with foil, and let rest for 20 to 30 minutes.

9. Slice into individual ribs to serve.

> **Change It Up:** This method for beef ribs works with any flavor profile, so you can add any type of sauce you like at the end, such as Korean-Inspired Barbecue Sauce (page 163).

Prime Rib

Prime rib is an investment we make maybe once or twice a year for special occasions. Make the most of it by cooking your prime rib on the grill. Live-fire cooking creates a nice, flavorful crust and imparts a slight hint of smoke that marries well with the meat's natural beefiness. *Serves 6*

PREP TIME: 15 minutes **GRILLING TIME:** 1 hour 40 minutes, plus 30 minutes to rest

- 2 tablespoons Dijon mustard
- 2 tablespoons olive oil
- 2 tablespoons kosher salt
- 3 garlic cloves, minced
- 1 tablespoon minced shallot
- 2 teaspoons minced fresh rosemary leaves
- 2 teaspoons minced fresh marjoram leaves
- 2 teaspoons freshly ground black pepper
- 1 (5-pound) standing prime rib roast

TOOLS: Aluminum foil pan

1. Preheat the grill for indirect cooking at 325°F, or medium heat. Set a foil pan under the grates of the indirect grilling area.

2. In a small bowl, whisk the mustard, oil, salt, garlic, shallot, rosemary, marjoram, and pepper to combine. Spread the mixture evenly over the surface of the prime rib roast.

3. Place the roast on the indirect grilling area, close the lid, and cook for about 1 hour 30 minutes, flipping occasionally, until it reaches an internal temperature of 125°F.

4. Move the prime rib roast to direct heat and sear it for 2 to 3 minutes per side, exposing it to the direct flame, being careful not to burn it; look for a rich brown color.

5. Remove the roast from the grill, tent it loosely with aluminum foil, and let rest for 20 to 30 minutes.

6. Remove the bone section, carve the eye of the roast into ¾-inch-thick slices, and serve.

> **Grill Like a Pro:** Save the drippings that fall into the pan, strain them to remove excess oil, and use the rest in your favorite gravy recipe or as a jus to serve alongside the meat.

Brisket

Brisket is considered the most challenging cut of meat to smoke. Although a classic, it can take the better part of a day to reach tender perfection if you're cooking it in a smoker. On the grill, we speed up the process by starting with a smaller brisket and using a few cheats. *Serves 8 to 10*

PREP TIME: 20 minutes, plus 1 hour to rest **GRILLING TIME:** 12 hours, plus 1 hour to rest

1 (10- to 12-pound) brisket

½ cup Central Texas Beef Rub (page 156)

TOOLS: Cherry, hickory, oak, or pecan wood

1. Remove the brisket from its packaging and place it on a large cutting board. Trim away the exposed fat. Season the brisket on all sides with a heavy coating of rub. Using clean hands, massage the rub onto the meat to make sure it is even and there are no clumps. Let the brisket sit at room temperature for 1 hour.

2. Preheat the grill for indirect cooking at 250°F, or low heat. Add the wood about 5 minutes before the meat goes on the grill. For charcoal, make sure you have plenty of hardwood chunks ready. For a gas grill, prepare at least 6 smoke packets or prepare your smoker tube or box.

3. Place the brisket on the indirect grilling area, close the lid, and cook for 3 hours, adding additional wood or smoke packets every hour. After 3 hours, rotate the brisket. Continue cooking and adding wood or smoke packets.

4. Once the brisket reaches an internal temperature of 165°F, after 5 to 6 hours, wrap the brisket tightly in aluminum foil and cook for 4 to 6 hours more, without adding more wood or smoke packets, until it reaches an internal temperature between 195° and 200°F.

5. Remove the brisket from the grill and let it rest in the foil for 45 to 60 minutes. Carve the brisket into ¼- to ½-inch-thick slices to serve.

   Grill Like a Pro: Once you've reached step 6, the brisket has absorbed all the smoke it can. After you've wrapped it in aluminum foil, you can remove it from your grill and finish it in a 250°F oven on a baking sheet.

The Lonestar Steak

The first time we tasted chipotle butter on steak, at one of our favorite restaurants in San Antonio, we realized it was the perfect pairing. The spicy, earthy chipotle adds exactly the right kick. *Serves 4*

PREP TIME: 15 minutes, plus 30 minutes to stand   **GRILLING TIME:** 15 minutes

For the Steaks
4 (1- to 1¼-inch-thick) New York strip steaks
2 tablespoons olive oil
1 to 1½ tablespoons Central Texas Beef Rub (page 156)

For the chipotle butter
8 tablespoons (1 stick) unsalted butter, at room temperature
1 tablespoon minced chipotle pepper in adobo
1 tablespoon minced shallot
1 tablespoon minced chives
1 tablespoon freshly squeezed lime juice
¼ teaspoon kosher salt
⅛ teaspoon freshly ground black pepper

TOOLS: Basting brush

1. Brush the steaks on both sides with the oil, then season both sides with the rub. Let the meat stand at room temperature for 15 to 30 minutes.

2. **To make the chipotle butter:** In a small bowl, use a fork to mash together the butter, chipotle pepper, shallot, chives, lime juice, salt, and pepper. Cover and reserve for serving.

3. Preheat the grill for direct cooking at 450°F, or high heat.

4. Put the steaks on the grill, close the lid, and cook for 5 minutes. Flip the steaks and cook for about 7 minutes, or until the steaks reach an internal temperature of 130°F for medium-rare doneness. Watch for flare-ups and adjust the heat, as needed. Remove the steaks from the grill and let rest for 5 minutes.

5. Serve each steak topped with a tablespoon or two of chipotle butter.

> **Grill Like a Pro:** Strip steaks generally have a strip of fat that runs along one side that sometimes includes a tough strip of connective tissue. This shrinks as it cooks and can cause the steak to curl. Cut through it at every inch before cooking to prevent curling.

Stuffed Leg of Lamb

One of our fondest food memories is the first time we tried the stuffed lamb leg served by vendors at our local Greek festival. It was a culinary masterpiece and the result of the cooks' many years of perfecting the art of cooking lamb. Our recipe is loosely based on that dish with a lemon-rosemary marinade and a stuffing of feta, herbs, and pine nuts. *Serves 6*

PREP TIME: 20 minutes, plus 3 to 4 hours to marinate **GRILLING TIME:** 2 hours

1 (3½- to 4-pound)
boneless lamb leg

1 cup Lemon and
Rosemary Marinade
(page 168)

¼ cup pine nuts

1½ to 2 teaspoons salt

¾ cup crumbled
feta cheese

1 tablespoon olive oil

1 tablespoon chopped
fresh oregano leaves

2 teaspoons fresh
thyme leaves

3 garlic cloves, minced

1 tablespoon freshly
squeezed lemon juice

TOOLS: Large glass baking dish, kitchen twine, and aluminum foil pan

1. Unroll the lamb leg. Trim away any large knobs of fat and tough bits of silver skin.

2. Place the leg, cut-side up, in a large glass baking dish. Pour the marinade over the top, making sure all surfaces are well coated. Cover the dish tightly with plastic wrap and refrigerate for 3 to 4 hours.

3. In a small skillet over medium heat, toast the pine nuts for 2 minutes, shaking the pan often so they do not burn. Once the nuts are fragrant and take on a light golden-brown color, remove them from the heat and place them on a plate to cool.

4. Remove the lamb leg from the marinade and use paper towels to blot off excess moisture. Season the outer surface with 1 to 1½ teaspoons of salt and the inside cut portion with ½ teaspoon of salt.

5. In a small bowl, stir together the feta, pine nuts, oil, oregano, thyme, garlic, and lemon juice. Scoop the mixture into the cut section of the lamb leg and lightly spread it out, leaving ¾ inch on either end uncovered. This will help prevent the filling from leaking out as it cooks. (Keep in mind that each lamb leg is different and might not be able to accommodate all of the filling.)

6. Gently reroll the lamb leg and tie it with kitchen twine to secure it.

7. Preheat the grill for indirect cooking at 325°F, or medium heat. Place a foil pan under the grates of the indirect grilling area.

8. Place the lamb leg on the indirect grilling area, close the lid, and cook for 1 hour 30 minutes to 2 hours, or until the internal temperature reaches 150°F, turning halfway through.

9. Remove the stuffed lamb leg from the grill, tent it loosely with aluminum foil, and let rest for 10 minutes.

10. Remove the kitchen twine and slice the lamb into ¾-inch slices to serve.

Tandoori Rack of Lamb

Tandoori is a South Asian cooking method wherein meat is marinated in a yogurt mixture, then cooked in a tandoor oven. But you don't need a tandoor to make tandoori-style rack of lamb—your grill will do a great job. *Serves 6*

PREP TIME: 15 minutes, plus 4 to 6 hours to marinate **GRILLING TIME:** 20 minutes, plus 10 minutes to rest

- **2 racks of lamb (3 pounds total)**
- **½ cup plain whole milk yogurt**
- **2 tablespoons freshly squeezed lime juice**
- **4 garlic cloves, minced**
- **2 teaspoons ground cumin**
- **1 teaspoon ground coriander**
- **1 teaspoon salt**
- **1 teaspoon freshly ground black pepper**
- **1 teaspoon grated peeled fresh ginger**
- **¼ teaspoon cayenne pepper**
- **3 or 4 drops red food coloring**
- **¼ cup chopped fresh cilantro**

TOOLS: Large glass baking dish and aluminum foil pan

1. Trim off any excess fat from the bone sections of the racks. Remove the thick fat cap on top of the meat. Using paper towels, blot the racks dry and place them, bone-side down, into a large glass baking dish.

2. In a small bowl, whisk the yogurt, lime juice, garlic, cumin, coriander, salt, black pepper, ginger, and cayenne to taste. Stir in the food coloring. Spoon half of the yogurt mixture onto the meat of each rack but avoid the bones. Cover the dish with plastic wrap and refrigerate for 4 to 6 hours.

3. Preheat the grill for direct cooking at 400°F, or medium-high heat. Place a foil pan under the grates of the direct grilling area.

4. Remove the lamb racks from the marinade. Wrap the bone ends tightly in aluminum foil. Discard the marinade.

5. Place the lamb on the grill, close the lid, and cook for 15 to 20 minutes, turning it often, or until the internal temperature reaches between 130°and 135°F. Watch for burning.

6. Remove the lamb from the grill, tent it loosely with foil, and let rest for 10 minutes. Cut the racks into individual chops and garnish with the cilantro to serve.

Lamb Rissoles

Rissoles is a popular meatball dish prepared worldwide. The meatballs are roughly the size of a slider burger patty and sometimes coated in bread-crumbs and fried, but we prefer ours hot off the grill. The base can be anything from potatoes to chicken and seafood. In Australia and parts of New Zealand, rissoles are made from ground lamb or beef, seasoned with a smoky barbecue rub, and grilled. *Serves 4*

PREP TIME: 15 minutes **GRILLING TIME:** 10 minutes

1½ pounds ground lamb
½ cup minced onion
2 garlic cloves, minced

2 tablespoons chopped fresh flat-leaf parsley, plus more for garnish
2 tablespoons tomato paste

1 tablespoon Magic Dust Rub (page 159)
2 teaspoons Worcestershire sauce

1. In a medium bowl, mix the ground lamb, onion, garlic, parsley, tomato paste, rub, and Worcestershire sauce. Form the lamb mixture into 8 equal-size patties.

2. Preheat the grill for direct cooking at 350°F, or medium heat.

3. Place the rissoles on the grill and cook for 3 to 4 minutes per side, or until they reach an internal temperature of 165°F.

4. Garnish the rissoles with parsley to serve.

> **Pair It With:** These little lamb patties go great with Eggplant Caprese (page 138) and Baby Potato Kebabs (page 146), with Grilled Peaches (page 151) for dessert.

CHAPTER SIX

Fish and Shellfish

Quick 'n' Easy Fish Tacos, page 117

Smoked Trout Dip

This recipe requires a three-step process, but it's well worth the effort. First, the fish is brined in a salt and brown sugar solution. Then, it is cooked low and slow for that smoky flavor. Finally, it is mixed with a creamy, flavorful mixture to create a dip. Serve this dip with crackers, chips, or sliced vegetables of your choice. We recommend using alder or maple wood for this recipe. *Serves 4*

PREP TIME: 15 minutes, plus 6 to 8 hours to marinate GRILLING TIME: 1 hour 30 minutes plus 20 minutes to rest

8 cups water

½ cup kosher salt

½ cup packed light
  brown sugar

1 (2-pound) whole
  rainbow trout

4 ounces cream cheese,
  at room temperature

½ cup sour cream

2 tablespoons minced
  red onion

1 tablespoon freshly
  squeezed lemon juice

1 tablespoon chopped
  fresh dill

¼ teaspoon
  garlic powder

¼ teaspoon freshly
  ground black pepper

Kosher salt

TOOLS: Alder or maple wood

1. In a large stockpot over medium-high heat, combine the water, salt, and brown sugar and bring to a simmer, cooking until the salt and sugar dissolve. Remove the brine from the heat and let it cool to room temperature.

2. Place the trout in a large bowl and pour the cooled brine over it. Cover the bowl with plastic wrap and refrigerate for 6 to 8 hours.

3. Preheat the grill for indirect cooking at 225°F, or low heat. Add the wood about 5 minutes before the fish goes on the grill.

4. Remove the trout from the brine, lightly rinse it with cold water, and use paper towels to remove excess moisture.

5. Place the trout on the indirect grilling area, close the lid, and cook for 1 hour 30 minutes, or until the fish reaches an internal temperature between 145° and 150°F.

6. Remove the trout from the grill and let it rest for 15 to 20 minutes, or until it is cool enough to handle.

7. Using clean hands, remove the bones and skin from the fish and discard. Flake the trout and set it aside.

8. In a medium bowl, whisk the cream cheese, sour cream, onion, lemon juice, dill, garlic powder, and pepper to combine. Fold in the flaked trout and season with salt to taste.

9. Taste the dip and season with additional salt, as needed. Serve immediately, or refrigerate for 1 to 2 hours before serving.

> **Flavor Boost:** For a little extra zing, add 2 teaspoons of Dijon mustard to the cream cheese mixture. You can also kick up the spice by adding 1 teaspoon of hot sauce.

Crab-Stuffed Mushrooms

These impressive-looking Crab-Stuffed Mushrooms are creamy and cheesy. The best part about this dish is that you can add ingredients to suit your tastes. This dish is designed as a main, but it also makes a great appetizer— simply slice the cooked mushrooms into quarters. *Serves 4*

PREP TIME: 20 minutes GRILLING TIME: 15 minutes, plus 7 minutes to rest

- **Olive oil, for preparing the pan**
- **4 medium portobello mushrooms, cleaned**
- **4 ounces cream cheese, at room temperature**
- **2 tablespoons mayonnaise, plus more as needed**
- **1½ tablespoons freshly squeezed lemon juice**
- **8 ounces lump crabmeat, precooked or canned**
- **2 garlic cloves, minced**
- **1 tablespoon chopped fresh flat-leaf parsley**
- **⅔ cup shredded white Cheddar cheese**
- **½ teaspoon Tabasco or other hot sauce**
- **Kosher salt**
- **Freshly ground black pepper**
- **½ cup panko breadcrumbs**

TOOLS: Aluminum foil pan

1. Preheat the grill for direct cooking at 350°F, or medium heat. Lightly coat an aluminum foil pan with oil.

2. Remove and dice the mushrooms' stems. Set aside. Use a spoon to gently scrape out the dark brown gills inside the mushroom caps and place the caps into the prepared pan, stem-side up.

3. In a large bowl, whisk the cream cheese, mayonnaise, and lemon juice until smooth. Fold in the crab, garlic, parsley, Cheddar, diced mushroom stems, and Tabasco. If the mixture is too dry, stir in 1 to 2 tablespoons of mayonnaise. Season with salt and pepper to taste.

4. Divide the crab mixture evenly among the mushroom caps. Top each mushroom with 2 tablespoons of breadcrumbs.

5. Place the pan of stuffed mushrooms on the grill, close the lid, and cook for 15 minutes, or until the mushrooms are tender but firm, the filling is bubbling around the sides, and the topping is golden brown.

6. Remove the pan from the grill and let the mushrooms rest for 5 to 7 minutes before serving.

Quick 'n' Easy Fish Tacos

To us, fish tacos mean summer vacations in the coastal regions of Mexico. Typically, the fish in these tacos is deep-fried, but we like to skip the breading and grill it instead. Our version yields a light and flavorful taco perfect for weeknight grilling or casual weekend gatherings. We recommend using a mild whitefish, such as halibut or flounder, for this recipe. *Serves 4*

PREP TIME: 15 minutes, plus 30 minutes to marinate **GRILLING TIME:** 15 minutes

For the fish
2 pounds halibut or
   flounder fillets
½ cup Mojo Marinade
   (page 169)

For the salsa
1 ripe mango, diced
¼ cup diced red onion
¼ cup chopped cilantro
1 tablespoon minced
   jalapeño

Juice of 2 limes
Pinch salt

For the tacos
12 corn tortillas

TOOLS: Large glass baking dish

1. Place the fish into a large glass baking dish, pour the marinade over the top, and gently turn to coat. Cover the dish with plastic wrap and refrigerate for 30 minutes.

2. **To make the salsa:** Combine the mango, onion, cilantro, and jalapeño in a small bowl. Add the lime juice and salt and mix. Cover the bowl and refrigerate.

3. Preheat the grill for direct cooking at 375°F, or medium-high heat.

4. Using metal tongs, dip a folded paper towel into the oil and rub the oil onto the hot grates to create a nonstick surface.

5. Place the marinated fish on the grill, leave the lid open, and cook for about 6 minutes. Flip the fish and cook for about 6 minutes more, until it reaches an internal temperature of 140°F. Remove the fish from the grill and cut it into small pieces.

6. Wrap the tortillas in foil, and warm them on the grill for 5 minutes, flipping halfway through. To serve, divide the fish evenly among the tortillas and top with the salsa.

Bourbon-Planked Salmon

One of the easiest ways to grill fish is by cooking it on a cedar plank. Planks help keep more delicate items, like fish, from falling apart on the grill, and as the wood plank heats up, it releases a small amount of smoke. Infusing the plank with bourbon imparts a nice earthy flavor. *Serves 2*

PREP TIME: 15 minutes, plus 30 minutes to soak the plank **GRILLING TIME:** 15 minutes

¼ cup bourbon, divided	1 (1-pound) skin-on	¼ teaspoon
2 tablespoons water	salmon fillet	garlic powder
Juice of 1 lemon	1 teaspoon salt	½ teaspoon chopped
1 lemon, left whole	¼ teaspoon freshly	fresh rosemary leaves
1 teaspoon olive oil	ground black pepper	

TOOLS: Spray bottle and 1 cedar plank large enough to accommodate the fillet

1. In the spray bottle, combine 2 tablespoons of bourbon and the water. Shake to combine. Spray the cedar plank with the bourbon water and let sit for 30 minutes.

2. Preheat the grill for direct cooking at 400°F, or medium-high heat.

3. In a small bowl, combine the remaining 2 tablespoons of bourbon with the lemon juice.

4. Cut the whole lemon into 3 or 4 slices, removing the pointed ends. Submerge the lemon slices in the lemon-bourbon mixture and let sit for 5 minutes, then remove the lemon slices and set them aside. Add the oil to the lemon-bourbon mixture.

5. Place the salmon fillet, skin-side down, on the cedar plank and brush it with the lemon-bourbon mixture. Season with the salt, pepper, garlic powder, and rosemary and arrange the soaked lemon slices on top.

6. Place the plank on the grill, close the lid, and cook for about 15 minutes, until the thickest part of the salmon reaches 145°F, brushing on more bourbon mixture, if you like.

7. Remove the plank from the grill and let the salmon rest for 5 minutes before serving.

Korean-Style Salmon Steaks

People often confuse salmon steaks and salmon fillets. The fillet is cut parallel to the rigid center bone of the fish, whereas salmon steaks are cut perpendicular to the bone. You can tell the difference if you look at the shape: The steaks appear large on top, with two small taillike portions underneath, and the fillet is one long strip of meat. Salmon steaks are often overlooked, but this cut lends itself well to grilling. This recipe takes this great cut to the grill by glazing it with Korean-Inspired Barbecue Sauce. *Serves 4 to 6*

PREP TIME: 15 minutes GRILLING TIME: 15 minutes

3 (1-inch-thick) salmon steaks	Freshly ground black pepper	2 teaspoons toasted sesame seeds
2 to 3 tablespoons vegetable oil	1¼ cups Korean-Inspired Barbecue Sauce (page 163), warmed	2 medium scallions, white and green parts, minced
Kosher salt		

TOOLS: Basting brush and 9 x 9-inch aluminum foil pan

1. Preheat the grill for direct cooking at 350°F, or medium heat.

2. Brush the salmon steaks on both sides with the oil, then season with salt and pepper to taste.

3. Place the steaks into a foil pan or a large foil boat (a doubled piece of foil with the edges folded upward to create a shallow pan-like structure).

4. Pour ¼ cup of warmed barbecue sauce onto each salmon steak, making sure it is applied evenly; refrigerate the remaining sauce for later.

5. Place the pan on the grill, close the lid, and cook for 12 to 14 minutes, until the salmon reaches an internal temperature of 140°F.

6. Just before removing the salmon from the grill, warm the remaining barbecue sauce in the microwave for 30 seconds. Remove the salmon from the grill and drizzle it with the warmed sauce.

7. Top with the sesame seeds and scallions to serve.

Mojo Salmon Fillets

We love pairing the flavor of salmon with a combination of citrus and garlic, which really makes this fish pop. These tender salmon fillets soak up all the sauce's flavor. When paired with a flame-kissed finish, these Mojo Salmon Fillets are undoubtedly one of the best main courses we've ever had. *Serves 2*

PREP TIME: 10 minutes, plus 1 hour to marinate GRILLING TIME: 10 minutes

4 (6-ounce) salmon fillets	**1 lime, halved**	**Orange slices and thinly**
¾ cup Mojo Marinade	**Fresh thyme leaves, to**	**sliced orange zest, to**
(page 169)	**garnish (optional)**	**garnish (optional)**

TOOLS: Glass baking dish

1. Place the salmon into a glass baking dish. Pour the marinade over the top, making sure the fish is well coated. Cover the dish with plastic wrap and refrigerate for 1 hour.

2. Preheat the grill for indirect cooking at 400°F, or high heat. Place the salmon on the indirect grilling area, close the lid, and cook for 5 to 6 minutes. Flip the salmon and cook for 5 to 6 minutes more, until the salmon reaches an internal temperature between 140° and 145°F.

3. Remove the fillets from the grill and squeeze fresh lime juice over them.

4. Garnish the fillets with the thyme (if using) and the orange slices and zest (if using) and serve.

> **Grill Like a Pro:** Salmon fillets may not be out at your store's fish counter. Ask your butcher or fishmonger if they receive whole salmon and if it's fresh. If so, they'll likely be able to cut them for you.
>
> **Change it Up:** For a different flavor profile, swap the orange slices, orange zest, and thyme for ½ cup fresh cilantro leaves, chopped, and 1 scallion, white and green parts, thinly sliced.

Tuscan Halibut Fillets

This Tuscan-inspired recipe dresses up grilled halibut with a flavorful Mediterranean tomato relish. Tuscan cuisine is not overly complicated; instead, it uses high-quality ingredients to enhance a main protein. *Serves 4*

PREP TIME: 10 minutes, plus 30 minutes to marinate **GRILLING TIME:** 15 minutes

For the fish
4 (6-ounce) halibut fillets
⅔ cup Lemon and
   Rosemary Marinade
   (page 168)
1 tablespoon olive oil

For the tomato relish
3 Roma tomatoes, diced
¼ cup chopped
   fresh basil
1 tablespoon
   minced shallot

1 tablespoon freshly
   squeezed lemon juice
1 tablespoon olive oil
Kosher salt
Freshly ground
   black pepper

TOOLS: Shallow glass baking dish

1. Place the fillets into a shallow glass baking dish. Pour the marinade on top. Gently turn the fish to coat. Cover the dish with plastic wrap and refrigerate for 30 minutes.

2. Preheat the grill for direct cooking at 375°F, or medium-high heat.

3. Using metal tongs, dip a folded paper towel into the oil and rub the oil onto the hot grates to create a nonstick surface.

4. Remove the halibut from the marinade, place it on the grill, leave the lid open, and cook for 12 to 14 minutes, flipping the fish once, until it reaches an internal temperature between 130° and 135°F.

5. Remove the halibut from the grill and tent it loosely with aluminum foil to keep warm.

6. **To make the tomato relish:** In a medium bowl, gently stir together the tomatoes, basil, shallot, lemon juice, and oil. Season with salt and pepper to taste.

7. Spoon equal amounts of the tomato relish onto each portion of fish to serve.

   Grill Like a Pro: Skip the grill grates and use a presoaked alder plank instead: Place the marinated fish on it, set the plank on your grill, and cook for the entire 12 to 14 minutes without flipping.

Sizzle-and-Sear Tuna Steaks

Tuna steaks are incredibly versatile and delicious, and they cook quickly. It only takes 5 to 6 minutes to cook them to a perfect medium-rare. These tuna steaks are seasoned simply, grilled fast, and served with a flavorful Board Sauce full of parsley, jalapeño, and garlic. Although most cooks serve tuna steaks medium-rare (at a temperature of about 115°F), please keep in mind that the USDA recommends cooking tuna to 145°F, or medium doneness. *Serves 2*

PREP TIME: 5 minutes **GRILLING TIME:** 5 to 10 minutes

2 (8-ounce) ahi tuna steaks	**½ teaspoon sea salt**	**Board Sauce (page 164), for serving**
1 tablespoon olive oil	**½ teaspoon freshly ground black pepper**	

TOOLS: Basting brush

1. Preheat the grill for direct cooking at 500°F, or high heat.

2. Using paper towels, blot the tuna steaks dry. Brush them with the oil and season with the salt and pepper.

3. Place the tuna steaks on the grill, close the lid, and cook for 3 minutes per side, or until they reach an internal temperature of 115°F. Promptly remove the tuna steaks from the grill and let them rest for 2 to 3 minutes.

4. To serve, slice the tuna steaks into thin (¼-inch) strips and toss the strips in the board sauce, or use the sauce as a topping.

> **Grill Like a Pro:** We recommend sourcing fresh sushi-grade ahi tuna for this recipe. If you have doubts about the freshness of the fish, cook it for a few minutes longer. Keep in mind that the longer tuna steaks cook, the tougher they become.

Blackened Cod

If you're looking for a quick-cooked cod that is loaded with flavor, this recipe is for you. We recommend using a cast-iron skillet for this recipe, as it provides the right surface to properly blacken the fish. The benefit of using your outdoor grill instead of your stovetop for this recipe is that all the smoky fried fish smell will dissipate quickly. For a fun fusion twist, top these fillets with Easy Red Chermoula (page 171) or your favorite fruit-based salsa. *Serves 4*

PREP TIME: 10 minutes GRILLING TIME: 10 minutes

4 (4-ounce) cod fillets	1 teaspoon kosher salt	½ teaspoon dried thyme
2 teaspoons smoked paprika	½ teaspoon garlic powder	½ teaspoon cayenne pepper
1 teaspoon onion powder	½ teaspoon freshly ground black pepper	1 tablespoon olive oil
1 teaspoon dried oregano		

TOOLS: 12-inch cast-iron skillet

1. Preheat the grill for direct cooking at 500°F, or high heat. Once up to temperature, place the cast-iron skillet on the grill for a few minutes to heat up.

2. Using a paper towel, blot the cod fillets dry.

3. In a small bowl, stir together the paprika, onion powder, oregano, salt, garlic powder, black pepper, thyme, and cayenne to taste, then season the cod with the rub.

4. Pour the oil into the skillet and let it heat up until it smokes lightly.

5. Add the cod to the hot skillet and cook for 5 minutes per side, until the fish reaches an internal temperature of 145°F, is opaque, and flakes easily with a fork. Leave it on a little longer if you prefer it crispier. Serve immediately.

   Pair It With: We love this dish with Maple-Glazed Carrots (page 140) and Portobello Mushroom Steaks (page 147).

Campfire Trout

We grew up in the Mountain West, where fishing for fresh trout is common. This is one of our favorite trout recipes to cook over a live fire. It captures that campfire experience we remember so fondly. *Serves 4*

PREP TIME: 15 minutes **GRILLING TIME:** 15 minutes

4 small whole trout (about 2 pounds total)	**Kosher salt**	**4 bacon slices**
4 thyme sprigs	**Freshly ground black pepper**	**1 tablespoon canola oil**
		Juice of 1 or 2 lemons

TOOLS: Toothpicks, grill basket (optional), and aluminum foil pan

1. Cut the heads and tails off each trout. Rinse the trout in cold water and pat them dry with paper towels. Place a thyme sprig inside each fish, season it with salt and pepper, and wrap each with a bacon slice, securing it with toothpicks.

2. Preheat the grill for direct cooking at 375°F, or medium-high heat. Place a foil pan under the grates of the direct grilling area.

3. Using metal tongs, dip a folded paper towel into the oil and rub the oil onto the hot grates to create a nonstick surface. Alternatively, oil a grill basket and secure the fish in the basket.

4. Place the trout on the grill, close the lid, and cook for 5 to 7 minutes. Flip the fish and cook for 5 to 7 minutes more, or until they reach an internal temperature of 145°F, the flesh is opaque, and it flakes easily with a fork.

5. Remove the trout from the grill and remove and discard the bacon. Gently open the fish, remove the thyme sprigs, and lift out the bones. Squeeze a little fresh lemon juice over each fish to serve.

   Flavor Boost: Combine ½ cup of melted butter, the juice of 1 lemon, ½ teaspoon of fresh thyme leaves, and a pinch each of salt and pepper. Refrigerate for 1 hour. Place 1 to 2 tablespoons (depending on the size of the fish) of the butter inside each trout before serving.

Grilled Swordfish Steaks with Red Pepper Pesto

Swordfish works well with most flavor profiles. For this recipe, we use lemon butter and a red pepper pesto. This fish makes the perfect main course for a dinner party but is easy enough for a quick weeknight meal. *Serves 4*

PREP TIME: 10 minutes, plus 30 minutes to marinate GRILLING TIME: 10 minutes

For the fish
4 (6-ounce) center-cut
   swordfish steaks
3 tablespoons unsalted
   butter, melted
3 tablespoons
   freshly squeezed
   lemon juice

Kosher salt
Freshly ground
   black pepper

For the red
pepper pesto
¼ cup olive oil
4 jarred roasted red
   peppers

½ cup walnuts or
   pine nuts
⅓ cup fresh basil,
   coarsely chopped
2 garlic cloves, peeled
Kosher salt
Freshly ground
   black pepper

TOOLS: Shallow glass baking dish and blender

1. Place the swordfish steaks into a shallow glass baking dish.

2. In a small bowl, stir together the butter and lemon juice; pour the mixture over the swordfish. Cover the dish tightly with plastic wrap and refrigerate for 20 to 30 minutes.

3. **To make the red pepper pesto:** In a blender, combine the oil, roasted peppers, walnuts, basil, and garlic. Puree until smooth. Season with salt and pepper to taste.

4. Preheat the grill for direct cooking at 375°F, or medium-high heat.

5. Remove the swordfish from the refrigerator and use paper towels to blot off excess lemon butter from it. Season both sides of the steaks with salt and pepper.

6. Place the swordfish on the grill, close the lid, and cook for 4 to 5 minutes per side, or until the steaks reach an internal temperature of 140°F.

7. Serve the fish topped with the red pepper pesto.

Lobster Tails with Herb Butter

Lobster is one of the easiest foods to grill. Like most seafood, it cooks quickly and benefits from a good coating of butter. Cutting the tails takes some practice, but once you get the hang of it, the process goes quickly. Our advice is to use a sharp pair of kitchen shears to cut through the shells. *Serves 6*

PREP TIME: 15 minutes **GRILLING TIME:** 10 minutes

6 (8-ounce) lobster tails

8 tablespoons (1 stick) unsalted butter, melted

¼ cup freshly squeezed lemon juice

2 tablespoons minced fresh chives, divided

1 tablespoon minced fresh basil

3 garlic cloves, minced

½ teaspoon salt

¼ teaspoon freshly ground black pepper

2 lemons, quartered

TOOLS: Kitchen shears

1. Preheat the grill for direct cooking at 375°F, or medium-high heat.

2. Using kitchen shears, cut through the shell, from the wide top portion of the tail to ¼ inch from the end of the tail. Do not cut through the meat.

3. Make ¼- to ½-inch diagonal cuts on either side of the shell, being careful not to cut the meat. Carefully part the shell, and pull the lobster meat out a bit so it sticks out of the top. Using paper towels, blot the lobster dry.

4. In a small bowl, stir together the butter, lemon juice, 1 tablespoon of chives, the basil, garlic, salt, and pepper. Brush the herb butter onto the exposed flesh of the lobster tails.

5. Place the tails on the grill, close the lid, and cook for 7 to 8 minutes, or until they reach an internal temperature of 140°F. The shells should be bright pinkish-red and the meat will no longer look shiny.

6. Remove the lobster tails from the grill, garnish with the remaining 1 tablespoon of chives, and serve with lemon wedges for squeezing.

New Orleans–Style Barbecue Shrimp

This dish has deep roots in Louisiana's Creole culture. In Creole cooking, barbecue flavor comes from a braising liquid of butter, spices, and beer. Normally, this dish is started on the stovetop and finished in the oven, but our grilled version adds a little live-fire flavor. Sop up the sauce with French bread. *Serves 4 to 6*

PREP TIME: 20 minutes, plus 30 minutes to marinate GRILLING TIME: 10 minutes

2½ pounds jumbo shrimp, peel left on

1 cup chicken broth or vegetable broth

¾ cup beer

8 tablespoons (1 stick) unsalted butter, melted

2 tablespoons freshly squeezed lemon juice

4 garlic cloves, minced

2 teaspoons Worcestershire sauce

2 teaspoons fresh thyme leaves

1 teaspoon sea salt

1 teaspoon smoked paprika

1 teaspoon freshly ground black pepper

½ teaspoon cayenne pepper

¼ cup chopped fresh flat-leaf parsley

TOOLS: Kitchen shears and 12-inch cast-iron skillet

1. Using kitchen shears, snip the shrimp shells, going along the back of the shrimp and stopping short of the tail. Remove the vein along the backs but leave the shells on.

2. In a medium bowl, combine the broth, beer, butter, lemon juice, garlic, Worcestershire sauce, thyme, salt, paprika, black pepper, and cayenne to taste. Add the shrimp and gently toss to coat. Cover the bowl with plastic wrap and refrigerate for 30 minutes.

3. Preheat the grill for direct cooking at 375°F, or medium-high heat. Place a cast-iron skillet on the grill and let it heat for 10 minutes.

4. Separate the shrimp from the marinade and pour the marinade into the skillet. Cook for about 5 minutes, stirring often. Add the shrimp and cook for 4 to 5 minutes, turning often, until they take on a pink hue and the sauce has reduced by one-third.

5. Garnish with the parsley to serve.

Jumbo Shrimp Skewers

The chermoula sauce is the star of this dish. Here, jumbo shrimp spend a short time marinating in this herby, slightly spicy, earthy-flavored North African sauce. Then, the shrimp are cooked hot and fast. We recommend threading five shrimp per skewer and serving extra chermoula on the side. This is a great cookout option, and these shrimp skewers make a flavorful appetizer (one skewer per person) or main course (two skewers per person). *Serves 4 to 8*

PREP TIME: 15 minutes, plus 30 minutes to marinate GRILLING TIME: 10 minutes

2 pounds jumbo shrimp, peeled and deveined

1½ cups Easy Red Chermoula (page 171), divided

TOOLS: Food-safe resealable bag; and 8 to 10 wooden skewers, soaked in cold water for 20 minutes

1. Place the shrimp into a resealable bag and pour in ¾ cup of chermoula. Gently massage the marinade into the shrimp, then seal the bag, pushing out as much air as possible, and refrigerate for 30 minutes.

2. Preheat the grill for direct cooking at 375°F, or medium-high heat.

3. Thread 5 shrimp onto each skewer. Do not overcrowd the skewers.

4. Place the shrimp skewers on the grill and cook for 3 minutes per side, or until the shrimp have turned a pinkish color, are no longer shiny, and have a firmer texture.

5. Promptly remove the skewers from the grill and place them onto a clean platter along with a bowl of the remaining ¾ cup of chermoula for dipping.

> **Grill Like a Pro:** If you're hosting a dinner party, we recommend pairing this main course with rice and Grilled Figs (page 152), without the ice cream or heavy cream that turns the fig recipe into a dessert.

Garlic Butter Cast-Iron Scallops

These succulent scallops are bathed in a buttery herb and lemon-pepper sauce. Because there is a sauce, you'll need to use a cast-iron skillet for this recipe. The benefit of cooking the scallops this way is that they cook quickly—these caramelized beauties go from the grill to the table in less than 10 minutes. *Serves 4*

PREP TIME: 10 minutes **GRILLING TIME:** 5 minutes

2 tablespoons olive oil	**5 tablespoons**	**2 tablespoons freshly**
12 large sea scallops	**unsalted butter**	**squeezed lemon juice**
¼ teaspoon salt	**1 tablespoon**	**Pinch red pepper flakes**
½ teaspoon	**minced shallot**	**2 tablespoons chopped**
medium-grind	**3 garlic cloves, minced**	**fresh flat-leaf parsley**
black pepper		

TOOLS: 12-inch cast-iron skillet

1. Preheat the grill for direct cooking at 425°F, or high heat. Place a cast-iron skillet on the grill and heat it until it starts to smoke, then pour in the oil.

2. Using a paper towel, blot the scallops dry, then season them with the salt and pepper. Place the scallops in the skillet and sear them for 1 minute per side. Transfer the scallops to a clean plate.

3. In the skillet, combine the butter, shallot, and garlic. Sauté for 1 minute. Stir in the lemon juice and red pepper flakes. Nestle the scallops back into the skillet and cook for 2 minutes, basting with the sauce until they have a nice caramelized color on top and slight cracking on the sides.

4. Serve the scallops topped with the parsley.

> **Grill Like a Pro:** Scallops cook very quickly, usually in just 4 to 5 minutes. Keep in mind that they can go from tender to rubbery in less than a minute.

Clam Pizza

The clam pizza was invented in the 1960s by Frank Pepe, who owned and operated a pizzeria in New Haven, Connecticut. He noticed that raw littleneck neck clams, a regional favorite, were growing in popularity with tourists and decided to incorporate this ingredient as a pizza topping. It was a great success. Today, this pizza has evolved to include additional items, such as bacon or pancetta. The mozzarella (and lack of tomato sauce) gives the pie a white color and its traditional name, white clam pizza. *Serves 4*

PREP TIME: 20 minutes, plus 1 hour 15 minutes for rising   GRILLING TIME: 10 minutes

1⅓ cups warm water

1 (7-gram) instant yeast packet (2¼ teaspoons)

1 tablespoon sugar

6 tablespoons olive oil, divided

½ teaspoon kosher salt

3½ cups all-purpose flour, plus more for dusting

2 (6.5-ounce) cans clams, drained

6 bacon slices, cooked and crumbled

1 cup shredded mozzarella cheese

½ cup grated Romano cheese

TOOLS: Rolling pin and basting brush

1. In a large bowl, whisk the warm water, yeast, and sugar to combine. Cover the bowl with plastic wrap and let rest for 5 minutes; the yeast should begin to produce foamy bubbles.

2. Add 2 tablespoons of oil, the salt, and flour. Mix with a spoon or rubber spatula for 1½ to 2 minutes until a dough starts to form.

3. Dust your clean hands with a little flour and knead the dough for 3 minutes. Poke the dough to check for readiness: If it rebounds slowly, it's ready; if not, knead it two more times and retest.

4. Coat the dough with a little oil, cover it with plastic wrap, and let it rise for 1 hour 15 minutes at room temperature, or until it doubles in size.

5. Preheat the grill for direct cooking at 400°F, or medium-high heat.

6. Split the dough into two equal pieces. Lightly dust a work surface with flour and place the dough on it. Roll the dough pieces into two 12-inch circles. Brush one side of each crust with oil.

7. Place the crusts, oiled-side down, directly onto the grill, close the lid, and cook for 3 minutes, or until the crusts brown slightly. Brush the uncooked sides with a little oil and flip the crusts over.

8. Top each pizza crust with equal amounts of clams, bacon, and the cheeses. Close the lid and cook the pizzas for 6 minutes, or until the cheeses melt.

9. Transfer the pizzas to a clean surface and let rest for a few minutes, before cutting each pizza into 4 to 6 slices to serve.

> **Grill Like a Pro:** If you have a pizza stone, put it directly onto the grill and use it to cook one pizza at a time—no need to flip the dough. If you would like to streamline your whole pizza-making process, use premade refrigerated pizza dough. You'll need about 20 ounces of dough to make two 12-inch pizzas.

Vegetables, Sides, and Desserts

Maple-Glazed Carrots, page 140

Grilled Corn "Ribs"

These corn ribs are, quite possibly, one of the most surprising trending recipes of late. When we first made this dish, we thought it was just hype. However, they turned out better than we could have imagined. Due to their smaller size, these "ribs" caramelized quickly on the grill, adding a rich sweetness to their flavor. *Serves 4 to 6*

PREP TIME: 20 minutes GRILLING TIME: 10 minutes

For the corn ribs
4 ears corn
3 tablespoons
  unsalted butter,
  melted
2 teaspoons paprika
1 teaspoon chili powder

½ teaspoon
  dried oregano
¼ teaspoon garlic
  powder
Kosher salt
Freshly ground
  black pepper

For the sauce
½ cup mayonnaise
½ cup Kansas City–Style
  Barbecue Sauce
  (page 162) or
  bottled sauce
¼ cup cotija, feta, or
  Asiago cheese

1. Shuck the corn and soak it in cold water for 20 minutes.

2. Preheat the grill for direct cooking at 350°F, or medium heat.

3. Using paper towels, blot the corn dry. Cut the tapered ends off the ears and the cut the cobs in half. Stand the cobs on their ends, and cut through the core of the corn, splitting it in half lengthwise. Place the cut side on the cutting board and cut the piece in half lengthwise again. Repeat with the other pieces.

4. In a large bowl, coat the corn with the melted butter.

5. In a small bowl, stir together the paprika, chili powder, oregano, garlic powder, and a pinch of salt and pepper. Season the corn with the spice mixture.

6. Place the corn on the grill and cook the ribs with the lid open for 8 to 10 minutes, until they're cooked through and have a nice golden-brown color, flipping to brown all sides evenly as needed. Remove the corn from the grill.

7. **To make the sauce:** In a small bowl, stir together the mayonnaise and barbecue sauce until smooth and drizzle it over the corn ribs. Top with crumbled cheese to serve.

Bok Choy with Sesame-Garlic Dressing

This dish of lightly charred baby bok choy is bursting with flavor. The greens are drizzled with a fantastic soy, sesame, ginger, and garlic dressing. It's a great side dish for year-round grilling. Serve it as part of the main course for the vegetarians in your group. *Serves 6*

PREP TIME: 10 minutes **GRILLING TIME:** 5 minutes

¼ cup soy sauce

¼ cup honey

¼ cup rice wine vinegar

4 tablespoons vegetable oil, divided

2 tablespoons toasted sesame oil

3 garlic cloves, minced

1 medium scallion, white and green parts, minced

2 teaspoons grated peeled fresh ginger

¼ teaspoon red pepper flakes

1 tablespoon toasted sesame seeds

6 medium baby bok choy

TOOLS: Basting brush

1. Preheat the grill for direct cooking at 350°F, or medium heat.

2. In a medium bowl, whisk the soy sauce, honey, and vinegar to combine. Slowly whisk in 2 tablespoons of vegetable oil and the sesame oil, whisking until the dressing is slightly thickened. Stir in the garlic, scallion, ginger, red pepper flakes, and sesame seeds. Cover the dressing.

3. Halve the bok choy lengthwise. Brush the cut sides of each bok choy with some of the remaining 2 tablespoons of vegetable oil, then immediately place them on the grill, oiled-side down. Leave the lid open and cook for 4 minutes, or until the bok choy have grill marks and appear slightly wilted.

4. Transfer the bok choy to a serving platter, grilled-side up, and spoon the dressing over them to serve.

> **Change It Up:** Grill the baby bok choy as instructed, but omit the dressing and top with Za'atar Veggie Sprinkle (page 160) instead.

Eggplant Caprese

We developed this recipe when we needed a delicious alternative to chicken caprese. The eggplant is slightly crispy and caramelized on the outside and tender inside. Grill this for lunch or dinner, or serve it as a side dish or appetizer. Double the recipe if you're serving a larger group. We also recommend looking for an eggplant the same size as the tomatoes and using fresh mozzarella cheese. *Serves 2 to 4*

PREP TIME: 15 minutes **GRILLING TIME:** 8 minutes

1 small eggplant

2 ripe tomatoes

8 ounces fresh
   mozzarella cheese

2 tablespoons
   extra-virgin olive oil

Kosher salt

Freshly ground
   black pepper

8 to 10 fresh basil leaves,
   coarsely chopped

2 to 2½ tablespoons
   balsamic vinegar

TOOLS: Basting brush

1. Preheat the grill for direct cooking at 400°F, or medium-high heat.

2. Cut the ends off the eggplant. Slice the eggplant, tomatoes, and mozzarella cheese into ½-inch-thick rounds. Set the tomatoes and cheese aside.

3. Brush the eggplant on both sides with the oil and season well with salt and pepper. Place the eggplant slices on the grill and cook for 3 to 4 minutes per side, or until they are tender.

4. Arrange the eggplant slices on a clean platter, layering each with tomato, basil leaves, then mozzarella, and drizzle with the vinegar to serve.

   Flavor Boost: Change the flavor with a fruit-based balsamic reduction: Mix 1 cup of balsamic vinegar with ¼ cup of jam in a small saucepan. Simmer over medium heat (do not boil), stirring, for 12 to 15 minutes, until the mixture thickens enough to coat the back of a spoon. Remove it from the heat, whisk thoroughly, and let it cool completely before using.

Cauliflower Steaks

These easy, grilled Cauliflower Steaks make a great side dish to pair with most grilled proteins. Because they are flavored with a barbecue rub, these "steaks" work well with low-and-slow dishes like Brisket (page 106). They can also be served as the main course for your vegetarian guests. *Serves 4 to 6*

PREP TIME: 10 minutes **GRILLING TIME:** 5 minutes

2 heads cauliflower

3 to 4 tablespoons olive oil

3 to 4 tablespoons Magic Dust Rub (page 159)

1 teaspoon kosher salt

¼ cup fresh flat-leaf parsley, chopped

TOOLS: Basting brush

1. Preheat the grill for direct cooking at 350°F, or medium heat. Line a large baking sheet with parchment paper.

2. Remove the green outer leaves from the cauliflower but keep the stem intact. Cut the heads into ¾-inch-thick steaks, cutting from the top of the head to the stem.

3. Place the steaks on the prepared baking sheet and brush both sides with the oil, then season well with the rub and salt.

4. Place the cauliflower steaks on the grill, close the lid, and cook for 5 to 6 minutes per side, or until they are tender and golden brown.

5. Garnish the steaks with parsley to serve.

> **Change It Up:** Season the cauliflower steaks with Quick 'n' Easy Sazon (page 161), squeeze fresh lime juice on them after they come off the grill, and garnish with chopped cilantro.

Maple-Glazed Carrots

Forget those boiled glazed carrots of your childhood. The grill improves the texture of the carrots and imparts that delicious open-flame flavor. You'll have perfectly cooked carrots in less than 30 minutes. *Serves 4*

PREP TIME: 10 minutes GRILLING TIME: 25 minutes

3 tablespoons unsalted butter	1 tablespoon freshly squeezed lemon juice	1 pound carrots
3 tablespoons pure maple syrup	1½ teaspoons chopped fresh rosemary leaves	1 tablespoon olive oil
		Kosher salt

TOOLS: Basting brush

1. Preheat the grill for indirect cooking at 350°F, or medium heat.

2. In a small saucepan over medium heat, melt the butter. Stir in the maple syrup, lemon juice, and rosemary. Simmer for 1 to 2 minutes, then keep warm until ready to use.

3. If you have a few thicker carrots, halve them lengthwise to match the size of the smaller carrots. Trim off the stems. Coat the carrots with the oil and season with 2 pinches of salt.

4. Place the carrots on the direct grilling area and char for 1 minute per side. Look for grill marks, but avoid burning the carrots.

5. Move the carrots to indirect heat, close the lid, and cook for 15 minutes, rolling and flipping the carrots so they cook evenly.

6. Brush the maple glaze all over the carrots and grill for 3 minutes, or until the carrots are fork-tender, before removing them from the grill and serving.

> **Grill Like a Pro:** You can simplify this recipe by cooking the carrots in a cast-iron skillet on the grill. Char them first by placing the carrots onto the grill over direct heat, then transfer them to the skillet. Cook over indirect heat until almost tender, add the glaze, toss to coat, and cook for 2 to 3 minutes more. If you'd like to add some heat to the dish, you can add 2 medium jalapeños, sliced, to the pan when you add the glaze.

Grilled Sweet Potatoes

This recipe follows a two-step process in which the sweet potatoes are parboiled and then grilled. Raw sweet potatoes take their sweet time to cook on the grill, and the longer they cook, the more likely they are to dry out—or burn on the outside while remaining raw on the inside. Parboiling reduces the chances that the potatoes will burn. Although this recipe includes delicious toppings, you can certainly serve the potato slices plain. *Serves 4 to 6*

PREP TIME: 25 minutes **GRILLING TIME:** 10 minutes

12 cups water

1 teaspoon kosher salt

4 medium sweet
  potatoes

2 cups ice

4 tablespoons (½ stick)
  unsalted butter, melted

1 teaspoon Za'atar
  Veggie Sprinkle
  (page 160)

2 tablespoons
  vegetable oil

½ cup crumbled
  blue cheese

½ cup chopped
  toasted pecans

1 tablespoon chopped
  fresh chives

TOOLS: Basting brush

1. In a large stockpot over high heat, combine the water and salt and bring to a boil.

2. Meanwhile, peel the sweet potatoes and cut them into 1-inch rounds. Fill a large bowl with cold water and 2 cups of ice.

3. Boil the sweet potatoes for 10 minutes. Drain the sweet potatoes and put them into the ice bath for 10 minutes to cool.

4. In a small bowl, stir together the butter and veggie sprinkle until blended. Cover to keep the mixture warm.

5. Preheat the grill for direct cooking at 375°F, or medium-high heat.

6. Drain the sweet potatoes, use paper towels to blot off excess moisture, then brush them with the oil. Place the sweet potatoes on the grill and cook for 4 to 5 minutes per side, or until they are fork-tender and have deep brown grill marks.

7. Transfer the sweet potato slices to a large platter. Drizzle them with the butter mixture and top with the blue cheese, pecans, and chives to serve.

Fully Loaded Zucchini Skins

If you have ever grown zucchini, you know these plants can yield a *lot* of squash. One can only make zucchini bread so often before burning out on this vegetable. Recently, we thought, *Why not use the potato skin concept for zucchini?* Truthfully, this recipe is more a cross between fully loaded baked potatoes and potato skins, using a creamy, cheesy filling and a crumbled bacon topping. *Serves 4 to 8*

PREP TIME: 20 minutes GRILLING TIME: 12 minutes

4 medium zucchini

10 ounces cream cheese, at room temperature

8 thin-cut bacon slices, cooked and crumbled, divided

2 cups grated Cheddar cheese, divided

¾ teaspoon sea salt

2 garlic cloves, minced

2 small scallions, white and green parts, minced

¼ teaspoon freshly ground black pepper

2 tablespoons chopped fresh flat-leaf parsley

1. Preheat the grill for direct cooking at 375°F, or medium-high heat.

2. Cut the ends off the zucchini and discard them, then halve the zucchini lengthwise. Cut off an ⅛-inch strip from the center of the zucchini's skin sides, so they will lie flat.

3. In a medium bowl, stir together the cream cheese with three-fourths of the crumbled bacon, 1½ cups of Cheddar cheese, the salt, garlic, scallions, and pepper.

4. Divide the filling equally among the zucchini halves, but do not overfill them. The filling should be slightly rounded in the zucchini boats. Top the zucchini with the remaining ½ cup of cheese and the remaining bacon.

5. Place the zucchini halves on the grill, skin-side down, close the lid, and cook for 10 to 12 minutes, or until the zucchini are tender and the filling bubbles around the edges.

6. Serve immediately, garnished with parsley.

Bacon-Wrapped Green Bean Bundles

Bacon-Wrapped Green Bean Bundles are simple to make and a nice change from asparagus (the vegetable you most often see bundled this way). The green beans make a delicious side dish for any occasion and a perfect choice for the bacon lover. For best results, use green beans that are all roughly the same length and width, so they cook evenly. *Serves 8*

PREP TIME: 20 minutes **GRILLING TIME:** 10 minutes

1 pound green beans, ends trimmed	**½ teaspoon garlic powder**	**½ teaspoon freshly ground black pepper**
1 tablespoon olive oil		**8 bacon slices**

TOOLS: Toothpicks (optional) and aluminum foil pan

1. In a large bowl, toss the green beans with the oil, season them with the garlic powder and pepper, and separate them into 8 even bundles.

2. Wrap each bundle with 1 bacon slice, placing the seam of the bacon on the bottom of each bundle to keep them together. (Use a toothpick to secure, if needed.)

3. Preheat the grill for direct cooking at 375°F, or medium-high heat. Place a foil pan under the grates of the direct grilling area.

4. Place the bundles, seam-side down, on the grill, leave the lid open, and cook for 4 to 5 minutes. Gently turn the bundles and cook them for 4 to 5 minutes more, or until the bacon is cooked and appears crisp around the edges. Serve immediately.

> **Flavor Boost:** To add a sweet barbecue finish to these bundles, brush them with your favorite glaze or our Rib Candy Glaze (page 166) a few minutes before they come off the grill.

Grilled Corn with Spiced Butter

This recipe is inspired by the flavors of Old Bay seasoning. Grilled corn is amazing on its own, but our version is slathered with a spiced butter. We recommend doubling the butter portion of the recipe and reserving half of it to serve with the cooked corn. *Serves 6*

PREP TIME: 20 minutes, plus 30 minutes to soak **GRILLING TIME:** 10 minutes

6 ears corn, shucked

5 tablespoons
  plus 2 teaspoons
  (⅔ stick) butter, at
  room temperature

1 tablespoon paprika

1 teaspoon celery salt

¼ celery seed

¼ teaspoon
  ground mustard

¼ teaspoon freshly
  ground black pepper

¼ teaspoon
  garlic powder

¼ teaspoon ground
  cinnamon

¼ teaspoon
  cayenne pepper

TOOLS: Basting brush

1. Cut the knob off the bottom of each ear of corn. Soak the corn in a large pot of cold water for 30 minutes.

2. Preheat the grill for direct cooking at 350°F, or medium heat.

3. In a small bowl, stir together the butter, paprika, celery salt, celery seed, ground mustard, black pepper, garlic powder, cinnamon, and cayenne to taste.

4. Remove the corn from the water and use paper towels to blot off excess moisture. Brush each ear with a thick coating of the seasoned butter mixture, leaving some to add to the corn once it is grilled.

5. Place the corn on the direct grilling area and cook until all sides have some light charring, rotating the corn every 30 to 40 seconds to sear the surface. Move the corn to indirect heat and cook for 5 to 7 minutes more, until tender.

6. Serve the corn with the remaining seasoned butter on the side.

> **Grill Like a Pro:** Add a hit of smoke by adding wood a few minutes before placing the corn onto the grill. We recommend cherry, pecan, or maple wood. You can also dust the corn with additional paprika or pepper, if you like.

Baby Potato Kebabs

Potato kebabs go well with most grilled proteins. The two-step process of parboiling and then grilling the potatoes ensures they end up soft in the center and slightly crispy outside. We recommend pairing this dish with the Reverse-Seared Tomahawk Steaks with Gremolata (page 94). *Serves 6*

PREP TIME: 15 minutes **COOKING AND GRILLING TIME:** 22 minutes, plus 15 minutes to cool

8 cups water

1 teaspoon salt

2 pounds mini yellow potatoes (about 30 total)

2 cups ice

8 tablespoons (1 stick) unsalted butter, melted

Grated zest of 1 lemon

Juice of 1 lemon

1½ teaspoons coarse sea salt

2 tablespoons chopped fresh oregano leaves

1 teaspoon fresh thyme leaves

½ teaspoon garlic powder

½ teaspoon freshly ground black pepper

TOOLS: 6 to 8 wooden skewers, soaked in cold water for 20 minutes

1. In a large stockpot over high heat, combine the water and salt and bring to a boil. Add the potatoes and cook for 10 to 12 minutes, or until they are nearly fork-tender.

2. Fill a large bowl with cold water and 2 cups of ice.

3. Drain the potatoes and put them directly into the ice bath for 10 to 15 minutes to halt the cooking.

4. Preheat the grill for direct cooking at 375°F, or medium-high heat.

5. Remove the potatoes from the ice bath and use paper towels to dry them. Return them to the now-empty pot.

6. In a small bowl, stir together the butter, lemon zest and juice, salt, oregano, thyme, garlic powder, and pepper. Drizzle the mixture over the potatoes and gently toss to coat. Thread 4 or 5 potatoes onto each skewer.

7. Place the potato kebabs on the grill and close the lid. Cook for 8 to 10 minutes, rotating the kebabs every few minutes for even cooking, until the potatoes are fork-tender on the inside and golden brown on the outside.

Portobello Mushroom Steaks

These Portobello Mushroom Steaks make a fine side dish, but they also make a satisfying main dish all by themselves. The best part is that they are cooked in just about 12 minutes. We serve them with Board Sauce for a taste explosion. Alternatively, you can serve them without the sauce and pair them with our Endive Caesar Salad (page 148). *Serves 4*

PREP TIME: 10 minutes **GRILLING TIME:** 12 minutes

4 large portobello mushroom caps

2 to 2½ tablespoons olive oil

1½ tablespoons red wine vinegar

1½ to 2 teaspoons Central Texas Beef Rub (page 156)

Board Sauce (page 164), for serving

TOOLS: Basting brush

1. Preheat the grill for direct cooking at 400°F, or medium-high heat.

2. Using damp paper towels, clean the mushrooms of any dirt. Carefully remove the stems and discard them. Using a spoon, scrape away the black gills.

3. Brush the mushroom caps with the oil and vinegar. Season them with the rub.

4. Place the mushrooms on the grill, stem-side down, close the lid, and cook for 5 minutes. Flip the mushrooms and cook for 5 to 7 minutes more, or until they are tender and cooked through.

5. Serve the mushrooms whole or cut into ½-inch-thick slices, and top them with the board sauce.

   Change It Up: These portobello mushroom caps make perfect hamburger patties. Omit the Board Sauce and put the mushrooms on buns right off the grill, then add your favorite burger toppings.

Endive Caesar Salad

This recipe pairs grilled endive with romaine, bacon, croutons, and Parmesan. This versatile dish can be served as a main course for lunch or dinner, or paired with grilled chicken, fish, pork chops, or steak. Endive offers a mildly bitter flavor similar to radicchio. It works well with creamy dressings and mellow leafy vegetables such as romaine lettuce. *Serves 2 to 4*

PREP TIME: 10 minutes, plus 10 minutes to soak **GRILLING TIME:** 10 minutes, plus 10 minutes to rest

4 medium heads endive

2 romaine lettuce hearts

Olive oil, for grilling

Kosher salt

Freshly ground
  black pepper

½ cup good-quality
  bottled Caesar
  dressing, plus more
  for serving

4 bacon slices, cooked
  and crumbled

½ cup seasoned croutons

¼ cup shredded
  Parmesan cheese

TOOLS: Basting brush

1. Halve the endive and romaine hearts lengthwise. Place them in a large bowl, add enough cold water to cover, and let soak for 10 minutes to remove excess dirt. Remove them from the water and use paper towels to absorb as much moisture as possible.

2. Preheat the grill for direct cooking at 350°F, or medium heat.

3. Brush the oil onto the endive halves and season with the salt and pepper. Place the endive on the grill, cut-side down, leave the lid open, and cook for 5 to 6 minutes, until slightly tender.

4. Brush the cut side of each romaine heart with 2 tablespoons of Caesar dressing. Place them on the grill, cut-side down, and cook for 3 minutes, until they have some slight charring and the leaves begin to wilt.

5. Remove all of the greens from the grill and let rest for 5 minutes.

6. Chop the romaine and endive into bite-size pieces and put them in a serving bowl.

7. To serve, add Caesar dressing to taste, along with the bacon, croutons, and Parmesan, and toss to coat.

Corn Bread in a Skillet

This Southern favorite is a must-try. We love corn bread because it is a versatile dish easily paired with barbecued meats or served as a snack with a little honey butter drizzled right on top. *Serves 4 to 6*

PREP TIME: 15 minutes **GRILLING TIME:** 25 minutes, plus 15 minutes to cool

2½ cups yellow cornmeal

1 cup all-purpose flour

3 tablespoons sugar

2 teaspoons
  baking powder

½ teaspoon baking soda

¼ teaspoon salt

1 cup 2% milk

1 cup buttermilk

2 large eggs

4 tablespoons (½ stick)
  unsalted butter, melted,
  plus more for serving

1¼ teaspoons
  vegetable oil

Honey, for serving

TOOLS: 12-inch cast-iron skillet and heat-resistant gloves

1. Preheat the grill for direct cooking at 350°F, or medium heat.

2. In a large bowl, combine the cornmeal, flour, sugar, baking powder, baking soda, and salt. In a medium bowl, whisk the milk, buttermilk, eggs, and melted butter to blend. Slowly add the wet ingredients to the dry ingredients and whisk until smooth.

3. Pour the oil into a cast-iron skillet and place it on the grill for 5 minutes to preheat. Use heat-resistant gloves to tilt the skillet to distribute the oil over the bottom.

4. Pour the corn bread batter into the skillet, close the lid, and cook for 20 to 25 minutes, until a toothpick inserted into the center comes out clean.

5. Transfer the skillet to a heat-resistant surface and let the corn bread cool for 15 minutes.

6. To serve, cut the cornbread into pie-shaped slices and top with butter and honey.

> **Flavor Boost:** Try a savory and spicy version of this corn bread: Omit 2 tablespoons of sugar and add 1 large jalapeño, seeded and finely chopped, and ½ cup of shredded Cheddar cheese.

Grilled Peaches

If you are new to grilling fruit, we recommend starting with stone fruit like peaches. Not only are they easy to grill, but the natural sugars in the fruit caramelize quickly, yielding a delicious flavor. Keep it simple and serve these peaches with a scoop of vanilla ice cream and a topping of your choice. *Serves 6*

PREP TIME: 10 minutes   **GRILLING TIME:** 6 minutes

3 large, ripe peaches
¼ cup packed light brown sugar
¼ teaspoon ground cinnamon

2 teaspoons walnut oil or olive oil
3 cups vanilla ice cream

Salted caramel sauce, honey, fruit-based balsamic vinegar, or another ice cream topping of choice, warmed, for serving

TOOLS: Basting brush

1. Preheat the grill for direct cooking at 350°F, or medium heat.

2. Halve the peaches lengthwise. Remove the pits.

3. In a small bowl, stir together the brown sugar and cinnamon.

4. Brush the cut sides of the peach halves with the oil. Put the peaches on the grill, cut-side down, leave the lid up, and cook for 2 to 3 minutes, or until the peaches have nice grill marks.

5. Flip the peach halves and spoon on the brown sugar mixture, dividing it equally among the halves. Cook for 2 to 3 minutes, or until the sugar melts.

6. Serve the peach halves topped with a scoop of vanilla ice cream and your favorite toppings.

> **Grill Like a Pro:** Ripe peaches are the best for grilling. If the color is a dark yellow-red, and there is some shriveling at the stem, they are perfectly ripe. If you're not a fan of fuzzy peach skin, grill nectarines instead.

Grilled Figs

Fig season usually falls between July and October, and while most people eat figs plain or in salads, we highly recommend grilling them. We skewer the figs, brush them with pomegranate molasses, grill them, then serve them with mascarpone cheese, honey, and mint. Pomegranate molasses is available in most specialty stores, grocery stores, and online. *Serves 4*

PREP TIME: 15 minutes **GRILLING TIME:** 4 minutes

10 large, firm fresh figs

⅓ cup pomegranate molasses

Neutral-flavored oil, for grilling (such as corn or canola)

⅓ cup honey

⅛ teaspoon ground cardamom or cinnamon

½ cup mascarpone cheese, yogurt, ice cream, or whipped cream

4 to 6 fresh mint leaves, finely chopped

TOOLS: 4 wooden skewers, soaked in cold water for 20 minutes; and basting brush

1. Prepare the grill for direct cooking at 350°F, or medium heat.

2. Cut the stems off the figs and halve each fig vertically.

3. Thread 5 fig halves vertically onto each skewer with the cut sides all facing the same direction. Brush the cut sides with the pomegranate molasses.

4. Using metal tongs, dip a folded paper towel into the oil and rub the oil onto the hot grill grates to create a nonstick surface.

5. Place the skewered figs on the grill, cut-side down, and cook for 3 to 4 minutes, until they get a nice sear on them. Remove from the grill and let rest for a few minutes.

6. In a small microwave-safe bowl, stir together the honey and cardamom. Warm in the microwave for 25 to 30 seconds.

7. To serve, gently remove the figs from the skewers and divide them among 4 bowls. Top with the mascarpone, warmed honey, and chopped mint leaves.

Blueberry Cheesecake Crumble Dip

This recipe takes the concept of smoked cream cheese to a new level by turning it into a fun grilled dessert. For this recipe, you will cook the cream cheese at a low temperature, 225°F. The objective is to slowly smoke or bake the cream cheese—not melt it. It should retain its block-like shape, but have a soft, creamy inside once done. To add a little smokiness, we recommend using a mild wood like apple. *Serves 4 to 6*

PREP TIME: 10 minutes   **GRILLING TIME:** 2 hours

1 (8-ounce) block cream cheese

4 tablespoons packed light brown sugar, divided

1½ teaspoons ground cinnamon, divided

3 graham crackers, plus more for dipping

1 (20-ounce) can blueberry pie filling (or your favorite fruit filling)

TOOLS: Apple wood (optional), 9 x 9-inch aluminum foil pan, and food processor

1. Preheat the grill for indirect cooking at 225°F, or low heat. Add the wood about 5 minutes before putting the cream cheese on the grill (if using).

2. Place the cream cheese in the foil pan. With a knife, make ⅛-inch-deep crosshatch marks on the surface of the cream cheese.

3. In a small bowl, stir together 2 tablespoons of brown sugar and ½ teaspoon of cinnamon. Sprinkle the cinnamon sugar onto the cream cheese.

4. Place the pan on the indirect (cooler) grilling area, close the lid, and cook for 1 hour 30 minutes, until the cream cheese is golden brown. Keep a close eye on the grill's temperature and try to keep it between 225° and 250°F.

5. In a food processor, pulse 3 graham crackers a few times to pulverize. Transfer the graham cracker crumbs to a bowl and combine with the remaining 2 tablespoons of brown sugar and remaining 1 teaspoon of cinnamon.

6. When the cream cheese has cooked, spoon the pie filling onto it and top with the graham cracker crumbs. Close the grill lid and cook for 25 to 30 minutes more, until the filling is bubbling.

7. Remove from the grill and let stand for 5 to 10 minutes before serving it with graham cracker halves for dipping.

CHAPTER EIGHT

Rubs, Sauces, and Marinades

Maple-Whiskey Sauce, page 167

Central Texas Beef Rub

This is a classic Texas-style SPG (salt, pepper, garlic) rub. Here in Texas, we believe in simple seasonings for beef. Each pitmaster has their specific ratio for an SPG beef rub. We have made it our business to develop the perfect rub proportions that complement the natural beefy flavor of large roasts. Central Texas Beef Rub is typically used on beef ribs, Brisket (page 106), prime rib, and steaks. *Makes about 1 cup*

PREP TIME: 5 minutes

½ cup kosher salt	¼ cup freshly ground black pepper	2 tablespoons garlic powder

1. In a small bowl, stir together the salt, pepper, and garlic powder.

2. Store in an airtight container in your cupboard for up to 1 year; use as directed.

> **Grill Like a Pro:** Because this rub can be stored for so long, you can make a large batch by multiplying the ingredients. Check the rub periodically, giving it a good shake to prevent clumping. To make scaling the recipe easier, just remember the proportions: 4 parts salt, 2 parts pepper, and 1 part garlic powder.

Poultry Seasoning

Typically, poultry seasoning does not contain salt. This makes it ideal for those planning to wet brine their chickens and turkeys. It's also a great option for those who want to control the amount of salt added to whatever they are grilling. We suggest using 1 tablespoon of rub plus ¾ teaspoon of kosher salt (or ½ teaspoon of table salt) per 1 pound of chicken. For example, a 4-pound whole chicken would need ¼ cup of rub, plus 3 teaspoons of kosher salt. If you plan to wet brine the chicken, use the rub only and no salt. The brine will provide the needed salt content. *Makes ⅔ cup*

PREP TIME: 5 minutes

¼ cup sweet paprika

2 tablespoons onion powder

1 tablespoon freshly ground black pepper

1 tablespoon ground mustard

1 tablespoon dried oregano

1 teaspoon garlic powder

1 teaspoon dried marjoram

1 teaspoon dried sage

1. In a small bowl, stir together the paprika, onion powder, pepper, ground mustard, oregano, garlic powder, marjoram, and sage.

2. Store in an airtight container in your cupboard for up to 1 year; use as directed.

Grill Like a Pro: When applying rubs to whole chickens and turkeys, get some of it under the breast skin and inside the bird's cavity. To do this, loosen the skin above the breast sections near the cavity opening. Use your finger to separate the skin from the meat and work the rub over the breast meat and down into the leg sections.

Magic Dust Rub

Magic Dust Rub is easily one of our favorite rubs to use on pork ribs and pork roasts. The rich, earthy flavors of the chili powder and cumin are offset by the sweetness of the brown sugar and the heat of the black pepper and cayenne. We've omitted the salt in this recipe, as some folks like to brine or marinate certain cuts of pork like loin roasts before applying a rub. Use 1½ tablespoons of rub per 1 pound of meat and ½ teaspoon of kosher salt (or ¼ teaspoon of fine salt) per 1 pound of meat. If you plan to wet brine your pork roasts, do not add salt to the rub. *Makes 1¼ cups*

PREP TIME: 5 minutes

¼ cup sweet paprika

¼ cup packed dark brown sugar

2 tablespoons chili powder

2 tablespoons ground cumin

2 tablespoons freshly ground black pepper

2 tablespoons garlic powder

2 tablespoons onion powder

1 tablespoon ground mustard

1½ teaspoons smoked paprika

1½ teaspoons cayenne pepper

1. In a medium bowl, stir together the paprika, brown sugar, chili powder, cumin, black pepper, garlic powder, onion powder, ground mustard, smoked paprika, and the cayenne to taste.

2. Store in an airtight container in your cupboard for 6 to 8 months; use as directed.

> **Grill Like a Pro:** Apply this rub anywhere from 2 to 8 hours before your meat goes on the grill. Wrap the meat tightly with plastic wrap and refrigerate until 1 hour before grilling.

Za'atar Veggie Sprinkle

This flavorful Middle Eastern–inspired spice mixture can be used in multiple ways. It can be a seasoning rub for all types of meat and fish, as well as a garnish for vegetables, dips, and stews. We recommend using this veggie sprinkle on Cauliflower Steaks (page 139). *Makes ⅓ cup*

PREP TIME: 5 minutes   COOK TIME: 5 minutes, plus 10 minutes to cool

2 tablespoons sesame seeds	2 teaspoons ground cumin	½ teaspoon freshly ground black pepper
1 tablespoon dried thyme	1 teaspoon ground coriander	½ teaspoon red pepper flakes
1 tablespoon dried oregano		½ teaspoon sea salt

1. In a dry skillet over medium heat, toast the sesame seeds, stirring the seeds with a spatula so they do not burn, until they are lightly toasted and fragrant. Transfer the seeds to a plate to cool for 10 minutes.

2. In a small bowl, stir together the toasted sesame seeds, thyme, oregano, cumin, coriander, black pepper, red pepper flakes, and salt.

3. Store in an airtight container in your cupboard for up to 6 months; use as directed.

   Change It Up: To amp up the flavor, use toasted seeds and peppercorns instead of the already ground spices. Substitute 1½ teaspoons of cumin seeds for the ground cumin, ¾ teaspoon of coriander seeds for the ground coriander, and ½ teaspoon of peppercorns for the freshly ground black pepper. Follow the toasting instructions in step 1 and use a spice or coffee grinder to pulverize the spices. Combine with the remaining ingredients listed in the recipe.

Quick 'n' Easy Sazon

This Latin American–inspired spice blend is used to season all types of fish, meats, seafood, and vegetables. The main colorant of this mixture is crushed annatto seeds, also known as *achiote*. Annatto adds a deep red color and a light smoky flavor to the rub. Achiote powder is available in most grocery stores, specialty markets, and online. You can prepare this seasoning mixture without salt, if desired, especially if using it on brined meats. *Makes 1 cup*

PREP TIME: 5 minutes

3 tablespoons achiote powder

3 tablespoons ground cumin

3 tablespoons ground coriander

1 tablespoon dried oregano

1 tablespoon dried cilantro

1 tablespoon onion powder

1 tablespoon garlic powder

1 tablespoon salt

1 tablespoon freshly ground black pepper

1. In a small bowl, stir together the achiote powder, cumin, coriander, oregano, cilantro, onion powder, garlic powder, salt, and pepper.

2. Store in an airtight container in your cupboard for up to 1 year; use as directed.

   Grill Like a Pro: For a more refined seasoning blend, place all of the ingredients into a spice grinder or small food processor and pulverize the mixture to your preferred consistency.

Kansas City–Style Barbecue Sauce

This rich tomato-based sauce has the three important components of true Kansas City barbecue: sweet, heat, and a little bit of tang. This recipe works well on pork ribs and barbecue chicken. It also makes a nice table sauce. We recommend it on Pulled Pork (page 83) as well. For a more refined flavor, make this sauce a day in advance and keep it refrigerated. Before using, heat gently until it's warmed through. *Makes 2½ cups*

PREP TIME: 10 minutes **COOK TIME:** 20 minutes, plus 7 minutes to cool

2 cups ketchup

¾ cup packed light brown sugar

½ cup apple cider vinegar

⅓ cup water

3 tablespoons paprika (not smoked)

2 tablespoons chili powder

1 teaspoon cayenne pepper

½ teaspoon garlic powder

¼ teaspoon salt

1 tablespoon unsalted butter

1. In a medium saucepan over medium heat, combine the ketchup, brown sugar, vinegar, water, paprika, chili powder, cayenne to taste, garlic powder, and salt and bring to a simmer. Cook for 2 minutes, stirring occasionally. Reduce the heat to low and simmer for 13 to 15 minutes more, stirring as needed, until the sauce starts to thicken.

2. Remove the pan from the heat and immediately stir in the butter. Let the sauce cool for 5 to 7 minutes before using.

3. Refrigerate in an airtight container for up to 1 week; use as directed.

> **Grill Like a Pro:** Why the butter? Stirring in a pat of butter at the end of cooking helps "silk" the sauce, giving it a deliciously creamy finish. It also tempers some of the harsher acidic elements, like the tomato and vinegar. The butter doesn't remove their flavor but helps blend them in with the rest of the ingredients, tying the sauce together.

Korean-Inspired Barbecue Sauce

This sticky, sweet, and spicy sauce is easy to make and packed full of flavor. Use this sauce on chicken, fish, pork, and seafood. You can even use it as a dipping sauce. Typically, we add crisp, refreshing grated Asian pear, but this fruit can be harder to source in some areas, so we have simplified this recipe. If you have an Asian pear, grate half and add it to the sauce. *Makes 1¼ cups*

PREP TIME: 15 minutes COOK TIME: 15 minutes, plus 5 minutes to cool

1 cup low-sodium soy sauce

¾ cup packed light brown sugar

2 tablespoons rice wine vinegar or sake

4 garlic cloves, minced

2½ teaspoons chili-garlic sauce (such as sambal oelek)

1 teaspoon grated peeled fresh ginger

1½ teaspoons toasted sesame oil

¼ teaspoon ground white pepper

1 tablespoon water

2 teaspoons cornstarch

1½ teaspoons sesame seeds

1. In a medium saucepan over medium heat, combine the soy sauce, brown sugar, vinegar, garlic, chili-garlic sauce, ginger, sesame oil, and white pepper and bring to a simmer. Cook for 2 to 3 minutes, stirring often. Reduce the heat to low and simmer for 6 minutes, or until the brown sugar melts.

2. While the sauce simmers, in a small bowl, whisk the water and cornstarch until the cornstarch dissolves.

3. Increase the heat to medium. Once the sauce starts to bubble, stir in the cornstarch slurry and cook for 45 to 60 seconds, stirring, until the sauce thickens.

4. Remove the saucepan from the heat and stir in the sesame seeds. Let the sauce cool for 3 to 5 minutes before applying it to grilled foods.

5. Refrigerate in an airtight container for up to 1 week; use as directed.

> **Flavor Boost:** Replace the chili-garlic sauce with the same amount of Korean gochugaru paste to give the sauce a spicy, smoky finish.

Board Sauce

Board Sauce takes its name from the fact that that is where it is prepared and used—on a cutting board. It is a great flavoring agent for beef roasts, chicken, grilled steaks, heartier fish, pork, and shrimp. Board sauces usually contain olive oil, herbs, citrus, and seasonings. We like to add a little spice to our sauce and recommend using a seeded serrano pepper. However, you can also use jalapeños or milder peppers, such as Anaheim or bell peppers. *Makes ½ cup*

PREP TIME: 15 minutes

½ cup fresh
  flat-leaf parsley
2 scallions, white and
  green parts
1 serrano pepper,
  or small jalapeño
  pepper, seeded

2 or 3 garlic cloves
1½ tablespoons freshly
  squeezed lemon juice
⅓ cup olive oil

¾ teaspoon kosher salt
½ teaspoon
  medium-grind
  black pepper

1. On a cutting board, chop together the parsley, scallions, serrano pepper, and garlic. Into the mixture, slowly drizzle the lemon juice and then the oil. Mince the mixture together with your knife, drawing the oil into the herbs and vegetables until it becomes a cohesive sauce.

2. Season with the salt and black pepper. Gently stir to combine.

3. Refrigerate in an airtight container for 1 to 2 days; use as directed.

> **Change It Up:** Change the flavor profile and make a chimichurri-style board sauce. Use the recipe instructions to prepare the sauce with ½ cup of fresh flat-leaf parsley; 2 tablespoons of fresh oregano leaves; 2 scallions, white and green parts; 2 or 3 garlic cloves; 1½ tablespoons of red wine vinegar; ⅓ cup of olive oil; ¾ teaspoon of kosher salt; ¼ teaspoon of red pepper flakes.

Basting Sauce

This butter Basting Sauce is great for adding a little extra flavor and moisture to grilled chicken and turkey. We recommend using a crisp, dry white wine for this recipe, like a pinot grigio or a sauvignon blanc. Although this baste calls for Poultry Seasoning, you can tailor it to your needs; just replace the rub with 1 tablespoon of another rub in this chapter or a store-bought rub of your choice. To use, baste turkey or chicken during the last half of cooking. Make two or three passes every 15 minutes until your grilled item is done. Discard any remaining sauce that has come in contact with undercooked meats.
Makes 1 cup

PREP TIME: 10 minutes   COOK TIME: 5 minutes

8 tablespoons (1 stick) unsalted butter

2 garlic cloves, minced

1 tablespoon Poultry Seasoning (page 157)

1½ teaspoons soy sauce

½ cup dry white wine

1. In a small saucepan over medium heat, melt the butter. Add the garlic and cook for 1 minute, until fragrant. Stir in the poultry seasoning and soy sauce and let the herbs and spices cook for 30 seconds.

2. Turn the heat to low and slowly pour in the wine. Simmer for 2 minutes. Remove the sauce from the heat, cover, and keep warm; use as directed.

3. Refrigerate in an airtight container for up to 10 days. Reheat on the stove-top in a medium saucepan until melted through.

   Change It Up: Slather this sauce on Grilled Corn with Spiced Butter (page 145) right before it comes off the grill.

Rib Candy Glaze

Candy glazes have grown in popularity lately, and some backyard cooks would choose one over barbecue sauce. Glazes offer a sweet, shiny candy coating to ribs and chicken. Typically, candy glazes are made with a combination of various fruit jellies, with spicy jelly thrown in for extra flavor. Please note that apple jelly and cherry jelly are not the same as jam, marmalade, or fruit butter. Jellies are clear and do not contain bits of fruit in the mixture. Search for them in the fruit spread aisle in your local grocery store. When in doubt, check online. To use this glaze, brush your desired amount onto grilled ribs during the last 30 minutes of cooking. If using the glaze on chicken, brush it on during the last 12 to 15 minutes of cooking. *Makes 1½ cups*

PREP TIME: 10 minutes   **COOK TIME:** 10 minutes

½ cup apple jelly	2 tablespoons distilled	1 tablespoon Magic Dust
½ cup cherry jelly	white vinegar	Rub (page 159), or your
½ cup jalapeño jelly		favorite bottled rub

1. In a medium saucepan over medium-low heat, combine the apple jelly, cherry jelly, jalapeño jelly, vinegar, and rub and bring to a light simmer. Cook until the jellies melt. Reduce the heat to low and simmer for 3 minutes. The mixture should be syrup-like and coat the back of a spoon easily.

2. Refrigerate in an airtight container for up to 1 week; use as directed.

> **Change It Up:** Kick up the spice factor by using habanero jelly instead of jalapeño. If you prefer a mellower Rib Candy Glaze, omit the jalapeño jelly and increase the apple jelly or cherry jelly to 1 full cup.

Maple-Whiskey Sauce

This versatile whiskey sauce is great on grilled chicken, pork tenderloin, ribs, and even salmon. This sauce has a tomato and pineapple base matched with the standout flavors of whiskey and maple syrup. We recommend using pure maple syrup instead of maple-flavored syrup for a cleaner flavor. *Makes 2¼ cups*

PREP TIME: 10 minutes **COOK TIME:** 15 minutes

- 1½ cups ketchup
- ½ cup pineapple preserves
- ⅓ cup whiskey, plus more as needed
- ⅓ cup pure maple syrup, plus more as needed
- ¼ cup apple cider vinegar
- ¼ cup packed dark brown sugar
- ½ teaspoon chili powder
- ½ teaspoon onion powder
- ¼ teaspoon garlic powder
- Pinch salt
- Pinch freshly ground black pepper
- 1 tablespoon unsalted butter

TOOLS: Blender (optional)

1. In a medium saucepan over medium heat, combine the ketchup, pineapple preserves, whiskey, maple syrup, vinegar, brown sugar, chili powder, onion powder, garlic powder, salt, and pepper and bring to a simmer. Cook for 2 to 3 minutes, stirring often.

2. Reduce the heat to low and simmer for 8 minutes, stirring occasionally. Taste for sweetness and whiskey flavor and adjust to suit your taste.

3. Remove the saucepan from the heat and stir in the butter until it melts. Let cool slightly, then transfer the sauce to a blender and process until smooth. Keep the sauce warm until you're ready to use it.

4. Refrigerate in an airtight container for up to 5 days; use as directed.

> **Grill Like a Pro:** Remember that it's best to apply warm sauces to foods on the grill. Cold sauces tend to drop the temperature of the meat as it cooks. If you prepare this sauce a day in advance, let the sauce cool completely and transfer it to an airtight container. Refrigerate until ready to use. Before using the sauce, reheat it on the stovetop.

Lemon and Rosemary Marinade

This is one of our all-time favorite go-to marinades for chicken, fish, pork, seafood, and vegetables. We regularly make different versions of this marinade using a variety of herbs, like tarragon and marjoram for a French flair or mint and parsley for a Middle Eastern flavor profile. We have chosen a classic Mediterranean approach for this recipe, and it is our favorite combination by far. *Makes ⅔ cup*

PREP TIME: 10 minutes

2 teaspoons grated lemon zest

½ cup freshly squeezed lemon juice

3 garlic cloves, minced

1½ tablespoons honey

1½ tablespoons minced fresh rosemary leaves

2 teaspoons minced fresh basil leaves or oregano

½ teaspoon kosher salt

¼ teaspoon freshly ground black pepper

⅛ teaspoon red pepper flakes (optional)

¼ cup olive oil

1. In a medium nonreactive bowl, combine the lemon zest and juice, garlic, honey, rosemary, basil, salt, pepper, and red pepper flakes (if using). Slowly whisk in the oil. Let the mixture stand for 5 minutes so the honey and salt have time to dissolve. Whisk once more before use.

2. Refrigerate in an airtight container for no longer than 24 hours; use as directed.

> **Grill Like a Pro:** Always zest lemons before squeezing the juice from them. There is nothing as arduous as trying to zest a deflated lemon. Also, remove only the yellow skin from the lemon and not the white pith underneath, which is bitter and can ruin marinades quickly.

Mojo Marinade

Mojo is one of the most popular Cuban and Caribbean marinades. It originated in the Canary Islands and has undergone multiple iterations. This mixture is credited with inspiring elements of Southern culinary traditions, especially barbecue sauces from Florida, Louisiana, and Texas. There are four basic ingredients used in mojo: citrus, garlic, herbs, and spices. However, mojo can vary from cook to cook, with some people adding spicy minced peppers, liquified lard, or olive oil. Our Mojo Marinade can be used to flavor chicken, fish, pork, and seafood. *Makes 1 cup*

PREP TIME: 10 minutes

Grated zest of 1 orange
Grated zest of 1 lemon
½ cup freshly squeezed orange juice
¼ cup freshly squeezed lemon juice

3 or 4 garlic cloves, minced
1 teaspoon kosher salt
½ teaspoon ground cumin
¼ cup olive oil

2 tablespoons minced fresh oregano leaves
2 tablespoons minced fresh flat-leaf parsley

1. In a medium bowl, combine the orange zest, lemon zest, orange juice, lemon juice, garlic, salt, and cumin. Slowly whisk in the oil.

2. Add the oregano and parsley and stir thoroughly to combine. Let the mixture sit for 5 minutes, so the cumin and salt have time to dissolve. Stir once more before use.

3. Refrigerate in an airtight container for no longer than 24 hours; use as directed.

> **Grill Like a Pro:** When using an acidic marinade, it is best to marinate your food in a nonmetal container like a food-safe resealable bag or a glass or porcelain bowl. Otherwise, the acid from the citrus will interact with the metal, imparting a metallic flavor to the food.

Pineapple Marinade

This sweet and umami-filled Pineapple Marinade combines the tenderizing power of pineapple and apple cider vinegar with soy and honey to form a Hawaiian-inspired flavor bomb. This marinade works well on all meats, including beef, chicken, fish, pork, and seafood. It's also tasty on vegetables. *Makes 2¼ cups*

PREP TIME: 10 minutes

1 cup pineapple juice

½ cup honey

¼ cup soy sauce

¼ cup apple cider vinegar

¼ cup vegetable oil

2 or 3 garlic cloves, minced

2 teaspoons grated peeled fresh ginger

⅛ teaspoon ground white pepper

⅛ teaspoon kosher salt

1. In a medium nonreactive bowl, whisk the pineapple juice, honey, soy sauce, vinegar, oil, garlic, ginger, white pepper, and salt to combine.

2. Refrigerate in an airtight container for no longer than 24 hours; use as directed.

> **Grill Like a Pro:** The primary enzyme found in pineapple, bromelain, breaks down during the canning and bottling process, becoming less potent. For that reason, we have paired the juice with apple cider vinegar to ramp up its tenderizing power. If you have access to fresh pineapple juice, we recommend using it in this marinade; just omit the vinegar. Marinate red meats, poultry, and pork for 1 to 2 hours, and fish, seafood, and vegetables for 15 to 30 minutes.

Easy Red Chermoula

Chermoula is a delicious North African condiment and flavoring paste for all types of fish, meats, seafood, and vegetables. This mixture combines lemon, herbs, spices, garlic, and oil. There are three main types of chermoula, including red chermoula, which contains spicier elements, and green chermoula, which is similar to the basic version but contains preserved lemons and spices. We are huge fans of this red chermoula and love to use it as a spice paste for jumbo shrimp or as a topping for steaks and other grilled meats. *Makes ⅔ cup*

PREP TIME: 10 minutes

1½ cups packed chopped fresh cilantro

¾ cup packed fresh flat-leaf parsley

8 garlic cloves, peeled

1 tablespoon freshly squeezed lemon juice

2 tablespoons paprika

1 tablespoon red pepper flakes

1½ teaspoons sea salt

½ teaspoon ground turmeric

¼ teaspoon freshly ground black pepper

½ cup plus 2 tablespoons olive oil

TOOLS: Food processor

1. In a food processor, combine the cilantro, parsley, garlic, lemon juice, paprika, red pepper flakes, salt, turmeric, pepper, and ½ cup of oil. Puree the mixture until smooth, then transfer it to a clean jar or airtight container.

2. Top the mixture with the remaining 2 tablespoons of oil, cover tightly, and refrigerate for 24 hours before using as directed. The mixture will keep, refrigerated, for up to 4 weeks.

   Change It Up: If you are not too keen on the peppery nature of this condiment, swap the red pepper flakes for 1 teaspoon of ground cumin and 1 teaspoon of ground coriander.

Internal Temperature Cheat Sheet

BRISKET	195° to 200°F
CHICKEN BREASTS	165°F
CHICKEN WINGS, LEGS, AND THIGHS	175°F
FISH (SALMON, HALIBUT, COD)	145°F
GROUND POULTRY (CHICKEN OR TURKEY)	165°F
HAMBURGER PATTIES	165°F
LAMB	135°F (medium-rare); 150°F (medium); 160°F (well)
PORK CHOPS, ROASTS, AND TENDERLOIN	145°F
PULLED PORK	200° to 205°F
STEAK (1 TO 2 INCHES THICK):	120°F (rare); 130°F (medium-rare); 140°F (medium); 150°F (medium-well); 160°F (well-done)

Measurement Conversions

	US STANDARD	US STANDARD (OUNCES)	METRIC (APPROXIMATE)
VOLUME EQUIVALENTS (LIQUID)	2 tablespoons	1 fl. oz.	30 mL
	¼ cup	2 fl. oz.	60 mL
	½ cup	4 fl. oz.	120 mL
	1 cup	8 fl. oz.	240 mL
	1½ cups	12 fl. oz.	355 mL
	2 cups or 1 pint	16 fl. oz.	475 mL
	4 cups or 1 quart	32 fl. oz.	1 L
	1 gallon	128 fl. oz.	4 L
VOLUME EQUIVALENTS (DRY)	⅛ teaspoon	——————	0.5 mL
	¼ teaspoon	——————	1 mL
	½ teaspoon	——————	2 mL
	¾ teaspoon	——————	4 mL
	1 teaspoon	——————	5 mL
	1 tablespoon	——————	15 mL
	¼ cup	——————	59 mL
	⅓ cup	——————	79 mL
	½ cup	——————	118 mL
	⅔ cup	——————	156 mL
	¾ cup	——————	177 mL
	1 cup	——————	235 mL
	2 cups or 1 pint	——————	475 mL
	3 cups	——————	700 mL
	4 cups or 1 quart	——————	1 L
	½ gallon	——————	2 L
	1 gallon	——————	4 L
WEIGHT EQUIVALENTS	½ ounce	——————	15 g
	1 ounce	——————	30 g
	2 ounces	——————	60 g
	4 ounces	——————	115 g
	8 ounces	——————	225 g
	12 ounces	——————	340 g
	16 ounces or 1 pound	——————	455 g

	FAHRENHEIT (F)	CELSIUS (C) (APPROXIMATE)
OVEN TEMPERATURES	250°F	120°C
	300°F	150°C
	325°F	180°C
	375°F	190°C
	400°F	200°C
	425°F	220°C
	450°F	230°C

Resources

If you love this book, then check out our website for all the latest in barbecue and grilling, including hundreds of recipes and reviews of all the latest grilling products: DerrickRiches.com.

Our friend Kevin Sandridge's barbecue podcast, *BBQ Beat*, digs deep into everything that happens in the outdoor cooking world. Give it a listen, we know you will love it: BBQBeat.com.

Keep up on everything barbecue and grilling with Greg Rempe's weekly *BBQ Central Show* podcast. If it happens in live-fire cooking, you will find out about it here: TheBBQCentralShow.com.

BBQ Guys is the internet's biggest online grill store. If you are looking for a grill, this is the place to start. You will find grills not available in most big box stores: BBQGuys.com.

The first name in kamado grills, **Big Green Egg's website** also offers recipes and cooking techniques for all brands of kamado grills: BigGreenEgg.com.

Kingsford, the first name in charcoal, provides all the tips and tricks to make the most of your charcoal grill, regardless of brand, style, or configuration: Kingsford.com.

Thermoworks manufactures the best instant-read thermometers on the market. Used by almost every professional chef, these are the thermometers and temperature-monitoring devices to own: Thermoworks.com.

The Spruce Eats' grilling section is a great resource for people just starting out on the grill. Use this guide to help get you started and follow the links for loads of additional articles on every grilling method: TheSpruceEats.com /how-to-grill-331526.

Weber is the biggest name in outdoor cooking. Their website is not only a great place to find some of the best grills and accessories on the market, but it's also a repository for hundreds of recipes and grilling guides: Weber.com.

Index

Acknowledgments

We want to thank Rockridge Press for this amazing opportunity! We also want to thank our supportive readers throughout our tenure in the industry, our many talented colleagues, and Zoë, for always being our source of inspiration.

About the Authors

Derrick Riches is a highly respected barbecue and grilling journalist, outdoor cooking expert, and industry consultant. He is best known for his influential site on About.com between 1997 and 2017. As one of the most highly regarded sources for outdoor cooking information, he has answered thousands of questions, written hundreds of articles, and explored barbecue in its broadest definition. Derrick has traveled the world, grilled on almost every conceivable type of cooking equipment, led classes, and judged the best barbecue in the world.

In 2017, he founded a new informational resource at DerrickRiches.com, branded BGDR (*Barbecue and Grilling with Derrick Riches*). His work remains prominent, particularly in his thought-provoking articles, engaging videos, and notoriously honest product reviews.

Riches has been featured in *The Wall Street Journal*, *Business Insider*, *The Washington Post*, on the BBC, and in numerous books. He has served as a spokesperson for the Hearth, Patio, and Barbecue Association and regularly appears on industry-related podcasts, webcasts, and radio programs. He currently resides in Austin, Texas.

Sabrina Baksh is a cookbook author, recipe developer, content creator, industry coach, and photographer. Her work has appeared in various online and print venues, including *Esquire* magazine, *The Spruce Eats*, SBS Australia (Sydney Broadcasting Station), WebMD, and DerrickRiches.com. She has traveled both nationally and internationally exploring spices, culture, and food history. Very passionate about food and flavor, Sabrina takes great joy in the creative process. She currently resides in Austin, Texas, where she enjoys the rich food scene and the best barbecue Texas has to offer.